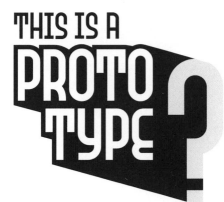

THIS IS A PROTOTYPE?

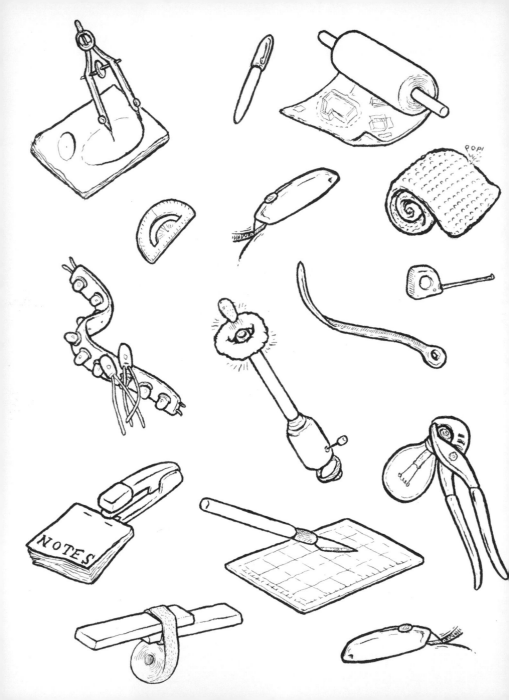

THIS IS A PROTOTYPE?

The Curious Craft of Building New Ideas

Scott Witthoft
Illustrations by Scott Teplin

TEN SPEED PRESS
California | New York

HASSO PLATTNER
Institute of Design at Stanford

240pt

Contents

41 pt

101pt

Sanchez Semibold 60pt

240pt

85pt

72pt

193pt

85pt

C:100 M:40 Y:0 K:20

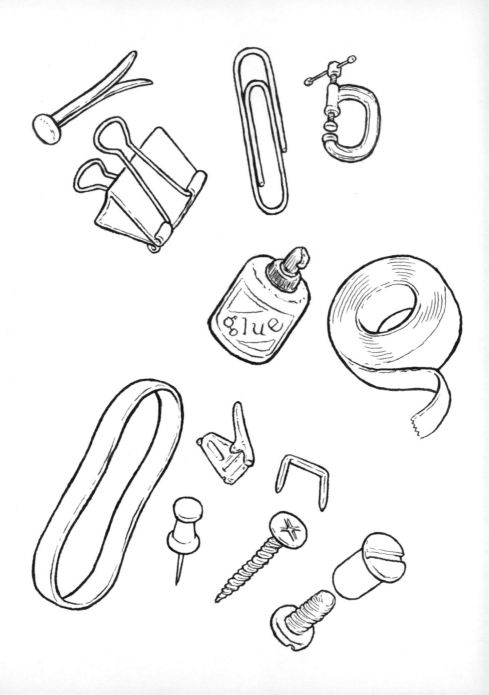

A Note from the d.school

At the Stanford d.school, *design* is a verb. It's an attitude to embody and a way to work. The core of that work is trying, to the best of one's abilities, to help things run more smoothly, delight more people, and ease more suffering. This holds true for you, too—whether design is your profession or simply a mindset you bring to life.

Founded in 2005 as a home for wayward thinkers, the d.school was a place where independent-minded people could gather, try out ideas, and make change. A lot has shifted in the decade or so since, but that original exuberant and resourceful attitude is as present today as it was then.

Our series of ten guides is here to offer you the same inventiveness, insight, optimism, and perseverance that we champion at the d.school. Like a good tour guide, these handbooks will help you find your way through unknown territory and introduce you to some fundamental ideas that we hope will become cornerstones in your creative foundation.

Put your gifts to use and lead with integrity in *Creative Hustle*. Find your voice and let it guide you with *You Need a Manifesto*. And in this book, overcome your ego and make your way through unknown territory one question, mock-up, and experience at a time.

Welcome to *This Is a Prototype*!

love,
—the d.school

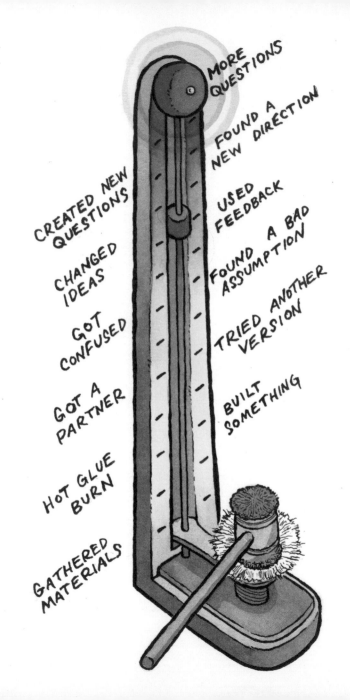

Introduction

How do you close the gap between *I wonder* and *I know*? You make a prototype. A prototype is a tool that gives you a chance to investigate your ideas and explore what could, should, or would come next, whether you are designing a new product, working out a new routine, or rearranging your furniture. It's a modest tool for the lofty goal of testing the future, or for at least testing a question you have about *your* future. Prototyping helps lower the stakes for exploring new questions by reducing risk—using fewer resources like time, money, and emotional commitment—especially when anxiety about outcomes might keep you from starting.

Prototyping is a primary tactic for designers, but it's a tool that also shows up in faraway fields. Skateboarders and chefs, for example, know that being intentional doesn't require being perfect at first. A skateboarder tries a new trick: that's a prototype experience. A chef experiments with a new recipe: that's a prototype experience. We know from watching both the skater and the chef that the next try comes after understanding what happened the first time. This is a strategy of repetition, not a singular performance. This is also a strategy of learning, with discovery embedded in every outcome. Through knowingly imperfect attempts, prototype experiences illuminate possibilities for your next move.

Unlike finished products ready for purchase, prototypes are imperfect and impermanent *by design*. Their value comes from efficiency, helping you learn the most from the fewest resources. This makes them a unique type of tool, such that the best prototype doesn't have to be of "best-built" quality right now.

The low-resolution nature of prototypes invites a behavior of breaking the things you make. Making and breaking is how you learn through experience. This means that prototyping is provocative by nature, with an undeniable element of fruitful sabotage. It's often misrepresented as an act of trivial trial and error or of recklessly moving fast for the sake of a crash. Sure, swiftness is a virtue, but a prototype's job is to teach from the broken bits, before fallout is let loose in the world. In some ways, that means prototyping is a slow art of figuring out by fumbling around; it takes practice to create prototypes that fail well.

This book presents tools, mindsets, and methods of prototyping that will serve your success no matter what project or product you undertake. Asking questions, speculating about answers, listening to responses, and understanding implications are all parts of an approach that we'll explore.

Prototyping is a reliable response in the face of the unknown in your career, your health, and your relationships. *What should I do? What is the right thing to do now?* These are common starting points. It's also common practice to seek answers in the same way you always do. What happens when you deliberately try to do something in a new way, one for which there is no known precedent? This is the perfect point at which to prototype—to skip past the fear of not knowing an answer and start with a question, without rushing to be "right," right now.

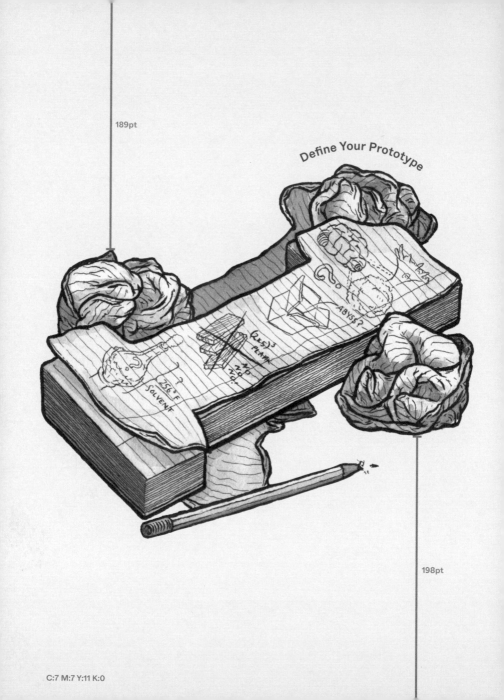

Define Your Prototype

189pt

198pt

C:7 M:7 Y:11 K:0

What Am I Doing?

What am I doing? Or what do I think I'm doing? This is the first thing to ask yourself on your prototyping journey. Without first being clear about what is right in front of you and what you might do about it, you will find that urgency, project pressure, and even your own expertise may cloud your way. Prototyping requires thoughtfulness right at the start, so answering this question will set your intention for the next step.

Giving a Prototype Definition

Let's create some clarity about what a prototype actually is. The word takes different definitions depending on the people and contexts involved. To someone prototyping a new diet, the word might mean trying out a new eating plan for a short time and then making changes based on how it goes. To someone sewing a backpack for the first time, a prototype might be a version that is a little messy and *will* require revision. At a company, a prototype might represent a trial run in a new market to see if there are untried sales opportunities. In each case, the word communicates different expectations and intentions.

What Is a Prototype?

What does the word *prototype* represent to *you*? Get a piece of paper and your most confident pen or pencil. Set a two-minute timer and write down a list of what you think a prototype is. To help you start, here's my own list of forty-two responses. Feel free to use any one of them as a launching point. Ready? Set? GO!

A model	Experiment
Sample	A low-res version
First attempt	Rehearsal

The cheapest way to do it

First draft

An outline

A road map

Mark I, II, III, IV . . .

Pseudo code

Simulacrum

An example

Dummy

Practice round

Proof of concept

Hero

Incomplete

Scrimmage

Junky copy

Rough draft

A try

Iteration

Alpha version

A hack

Beta version

Trial run

A test

Quick embodiment

Croquis

A Frankenstein

A "looks like" model

Nonfunctioning version

A mock-up

Schematic

Idealization

Template

Maquette

Cobbled-together concept

A stunt double

Pressure test

What Did You Notice About Your Definitions?

A prototype is an object or a physical thing that you might build or use. It can also be a concept or an idea. Any of these could inform a solution based on some objective. Did you find yourself wanting to add more detail? So did I.

A prototype's meaning takes a different shape based on what you're asking. That is, there is a question behind everything you build, based on what you are trying to learn and who you are engaging. It embodies a statement and asks a question.

I make a rough draft before I do a more refined version. (Did it with this book, too.) People make models to show others what an early version of something might look like. It's audience-dependent: *this* for one group and *that* for another. It's a practice run at home, but it's a pilot program at work.

Why a Prototype?

What does a prototype do? Why do we make prototypes? These questions ask us to look more closely at what it means *to prototype.* If someone walked into a room and caught you in the midst of prototyping, how would you describe the *what* and *why* behind your actions? You've just returned from an afternoon of prototyping: why were you doing whatever you did?

Try another two-minute challenge, with a subtle and significant change to the original question: What does it mean *to prototype* something? (The verb, not the noun.) Let that sink in. Now, GO.

To prototype might mean to (from my two-minute list):

Make an early version.

Try and see if something will work.

Show an early version to someone.

Test a concept.

A/B evaluate something.

Use rough materials.

Explore possibilities.

Get something right.

Check for imperfections early.

Validate an idea.

Be efficient early on.

Get feedback.

Show progress.

Ask a question.

Convince someone that something will work.

Be curious.

Communicate an idea.

Build something quickly.

Use low-cost materials.

Not worry about details.

Did You Notice That Action and Intent Emerge?

Making prototypes connects a question to an intent. Is this a way to achieve a goal? Will this concept create a new alternative? Just as with the previous list, some real-time themes popped up while generating this list. We see that *to prototype* is active—it's a verb. That's different from the

definitions in the previous list, which expressed a prototype as a thing—a noun. Both are true, and each has a
different implication.

A **prototype** is something you build or use. You can poke
it, start it, break it, measure it, photograph it—whatever.
To **prototype** is to cast a thing into action. The act of
prototyping elevates a stationary thing or idea into an
experience involving creation, adjustment, and understanding. That's not just a grammar game. It's a big deal
to recognize that your learning will come from thinking
beyond "thing."

How Is a Prototype Used?

How do you use a prototype? How do you test a prototype?
A prototype is always experiential. You make a thing, you
test that thing by putting it into action, and by doing so
you create a prototype experience. As an experience, a prototype opens up possibilities for understanding that aren't
obvious through thinking or imagination alone. This is a
dynamic and dramatic act, because turning a question into
an experience in order to understand the unknown is *huge.*

Purin Phanichphant, an installation artist and educator,
explicitly connects the word *experience* with *prototype*
from the start in his own practice. He explains,

> *Sometimes I am so focused on creating the prototype*
> *without realizing the question it's trying to answer.*
> *It's totally up to the designer or the artist to zoom out*
> *and see the full context. I have numerous students in*

my design classes who go straight to making wire-frames and interface click-throughs when they hear the word prototype, *without considering what happens before and after one interacts with the app. My cure for this is to use the term* experience prototype, *to remind them that there is a bigger picture, and to encourage them to role-play the total experience of the product or service.*

That profound perspective applies to all contexts, not just product design, and to ideas of all sizes across the spectrum of personal and professional life.

Creating an experience can happen in a flash when you're doing something fun and familiar. For example, laying out outfit options to wear on a date—this is an experience where you've asked and answered a question through action. It can take more time when venturing into the uncertain, such as prototyping a path toward a new career. Even when creating an experience does feel like instinct, it is worth understanding and exploring each element ahead of time so you're comfortable prototyping when the context is unfamiliar.

Designing What You Define

The pieces and process of prototyping are often part of technical vocabulary, which can be intimidating. But prototyping is an everyday practice that's a perfect fit for any moment when your curiosity meets an intention. Defining your prototype and considering the prototype experience from the start is effort well spent in developing the confidence to answer the big question: *What am I doing?* As you approach your prototype experience, there are three key elements to keep in mind that will keep you on track.

Identify Your Objectives

Prototypes usually begin when you have an idea in response to some situation—say, a robot that will help someone water their plants, or an app that will remind me to take my medications on time. Each of these ideas starts to give shape to a possible solution, but they are both examples in service of objectives—the fundamental motivations being explored. An early prototype may feel like a solution from the start, but it will reveal much more complexity once you explore it. At the start, state an objective for yourself: *Here is what I'm making, and here is what I want to learn from it.* This sharp clarity helps you avoid jumping to conclusions before you actually know what you need to accomplish. Remember, prototypes are tools to explore your objectives, not answers to questions you haven't yet asked.

When you ask *Why?* or *What am I doing?* with a new idea, you are focusing on what you hope to learn through what you make. What question are you answering by asking with a prototype. For example:

Does building bat houses help to lower the mosquito population in my yard?

Does this recipe get people to eat more vegetables?

Does this new route to work help me feel more
focused during the day?

Did this phone interview help a candidate feel
better about the hiring process?

Within each of these questions is a learning goal linked
to an assumption that a prototype *is* a possible solution.
A simple yes or no response to any of these questions is
actually unhelpful if the learning objective is to understand
why that was successful or unsuccessful.

Your prototypes and objectives *will* change based on what
you learn along the way. And as you start testing your
prototypes, it can be hard to separate solutions from your
original objectives. That comes from the familiar feeling
of falling in love with an idea before you understand it. It's
safer to fall in love with learning than it is to put yourself
in a position of defending an idea you haven't explored.
Try on this one: the perfect pants for any occasion! Who
wouldn't love that? Probably lots and lots of people, which
you might find out only after making countless versions
with no success. Support your early enthusiasm with a
pragmatic practice: distinguish your early idea—the perfect pants—from the objective: helping someone transition
easily from one occasion to the next. If you understand
your objectives from the start, it's less likely you will feel
trapped by the first versions of your ideas. Instead, you
can view your prototypes as perfectly imperfect tools for
moving toward solutions you have yet to imagine.

WHO IS THE USER? WHAT ARE THE GOALS? WHAT ACTIVITIES DOES THE PROTOTYPE SUPPORT? WHAT ARE THE KEY FUNCTIONALITIES? WHERE WILL THE PROTOTYPE BE USED? WHAT ARE THE KEY FEATURES? WHAT MATERIALS WORK BEST? WHAT ARE THE MOST IMPORTANT USE CASES? WHAT ARE THE KEY INTERACTIONS?

Catalog Your Curiosity

Creating a list of questions may not feel like a familiar first step in actually building something, but it is a great way to start. Artists, craftspeople, and designers constantly shift between making things and asking *why?* A prototyping mindset suggests that you are aware of both steps and are clear about when to focus on one versus the other.

Cataloging questions is not a hypothetical activity, so write down your questions for real. Use a spreadsheet, longhand notes in a logbook, or sticky notes all over a wall— whatever helps you organize your thoughts. Include basic details of time and place as well as abstract questions about how people react or identify their values.

Jon Freach is a design researcher and educator who routinely prepares for fieldwork and observation by starting with a template of default questions. Look to his list as a way to get started:

Who is the user?

What are the goals?

What activities does the prototype support?

Where will the prototype be used?

What are the key features?

What are the key functionalities?

What are the most important use cases?

What are the key interactions?

What materials will work best?

To take this further, expand your questions into categories based on your objectives. Three useful examples are *functional* (the practical details), *cognitive* (how your prototype will be understood), and *emotional* (the feelings connected to your prototype).

Some of your questions may be about the prototype itself—the thing—and some may be about the outcomes when someone engages with the thing or situation—the prototype experience. It is okay to have both varieties in your big list of questions to start. The benefit of beginning with a list is being able to navigate what to ask now and what to save for later, since not every experience needs to (or can) answer every question. You have license to prioritize importance by asking yourself: *Is this a question for now, or is there something more important I should explore first?*

Proto Your Type

Prototypes need to be designed. It may seem strange to think of designing something that isn't itself a solution, but a prototype is an unlikely product that calls for consideration. A trial run or a mockup is an abstract concept in service of something yet to come, but as a prototype it isn't abstract. You need to give it form, function, and flow.

Technical fields often use specific terminology to describe the purpose or variety of a prototype. That shared language helps people communicate with each other about what to make and what not to make. Prototypes fit into different categories based on different motivations. Each one may be more (or less) useful in answering a question that is important to you. These varieties often relate to physical versions of products, but they also apply to services and experiences that you want to try.

Just as you defined an objective with your prototype, you should also have an idea of what *type* of prototype you might use to get started. This sets the basis for what you want to learn from it. For example, if you are focusing on how something works mechanically, you might start with a *functional prototype* that pays less attention to the aesthetics of an experience. Your intent will help you decide how to start. Here are some common categories, with descriptions to help you choose a direction.

Prototypes Based on Utility

"Looks like" or aesthetic prototype. Shows how a thing or concept might look without having primary concern for the mechanical function.

"Works like" or working prototype. Informs how a concept might achieve a desired function, without direct concern for form factor or appearance. (This is often called a "Frankenstein" model, referencing the not-so-good doctor's bricolage monster.)

Functional prototype. Reflects evolved visual and functional characteristics close to a preproduction version. (This is sometimes described as a "working prototype," which can be confusing without context.)

Minimum viable product (MVP). Represents a concept (whether a physical or digital product) with the bare minimum needed to be released for testing with people. MVP comes from the lean-startup business practice of having an early, fully functional concept that can be tested and adjusted in the field. You can easily replace *product* with *prototype*—in this case to help envision the quickest, easiest way to build a starting point from a combined "looks like" and "works like" example.

Prototypes Based on Your Motivations

Prototyping to validate. Prototyping and testing to confirm whether you should advance an idea to a next step—which is often investigating market demand for the concept being evaluated.

Prototyping to decide. An exercise in creating prototyping experiences in which a team (or individual) evaluates single or multiple concepts in order to advance one concept and reject another—very often used among teams who have differing opinions about the merits of an idea. This method also resolves hypothetical disputes with help from actual results.

Prototyping to differentiate. A/B testing presents participants with almost identical prototypes save for a single variable (often a product feature) that shows up differently for user A and user B. The results can help evaluate the functionality and desirability of specific attributes.

Prototyping to explore. An experience mostly focused on behaviors or responses to an activity. This discovery approach often comes before you have any "looks like" or "works like" version of an idea in mind. Early reactions inspire options to make and try later.

These types of prototypes are meant to illustrate useful goals and benchmarks rather than rigid definitions. There's no need to feel beholden to any of them or obligated to memorize all of them; rather, you can work confidently, knowing that you can tune the form of your prototyping to a particular curiosity as you like. Sometimes it is just as helpful to rule out one direction as it is to choose another. Whatever choice you make should reflect your goal: *What do I want to know? What do I think I need to know next?*

Instead of seeing prototypes as solutions-in-waiting, consider them as concepts in service of your curiosity. This might be the first time you've made or embodied an idea outside of your head. An externalized idea! Your curiosity in exploring that concept is going to inform the real solutions. Starting with any concept, you will generate more new ideas and even more questions. By evaluating one idea, you will learn about the motivations behind that idea . . . only to discover that the question you thought you were answering with this "solution" is different than you imagined it. This is an exciting tug-of-war between being curious and being correct about your first idea. To start, focus on your curiosity as a guiding force for your exploration.

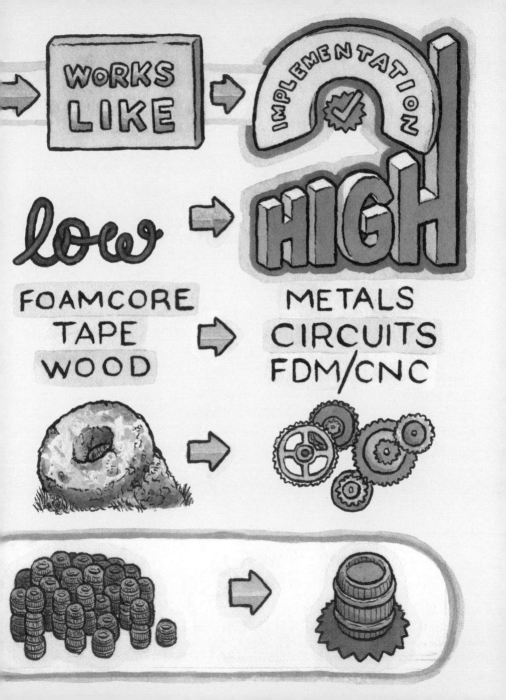

Making with a Mindset

Develop a few mindsets for putting all your prototyping decisions into action. That's an almost too-quick way to capture the breadth of concepts you've considered up to this point, but it's not at all trivial. Being comfortable with *how* you do your work is a significant benchmark in navigating the challenges you'll face when you move onto topics you've never explored or instances where you've never considered prototyping as an option.

When you start doing something uncomfortable or new, details can demand more attention, distracting you from focusing on your motivations. Early questions that feel like they call for immediate answers include:

What tools should I use?

How many prototypes are enough?

How will I know when I'm done?

Using a few mindsets to establish a protocol will help you figure out or improvise your way through those details as you deem them important or not. Try these three mindsets to guide your practice:

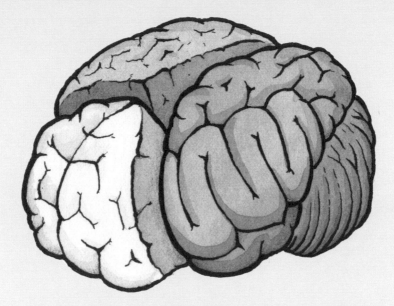

1 Make do by using nothing more than is needed.

The prototyper's art is one of making the most out of the least. The essence of the experience depends on establishing only a few details while allowing the rest to come from context and creativity in the moment. Two tactics you can use are (1) editing down to some basic elements as part of a prototype experience and (2) restraining yourself from overpreparing for every contingency.

Choose your basic details based on the core question you are asking, and save the rest for later. That's an intentional measure of restraint to help you feel comfortable when the experiences deviate from what you thought might happen and what really happens once other people get involved. Have you ever planned or participated in a picnic? That's an event that relies on only a few key details to start and becomes a success through workarounds and surprise improvisation. If you find yourself fretting over details or getting too specific, remind yourself to *make it a picnic*—match the resources at hand with the question you are hoping to ask.

2   **Make it fake, but do it for real.**

Create prototypes as physically and conceptually "big" as you can. You are trying to make the conceivable believable. Focus on emulating full-scale work, while keeping a limit on your time and resources. A few distilled details can make an experience feel real and immersive, just like a theater set from a play.

The closer your prototype comes to reality, the better you will be able to understand someone's true reactions and behaviors. Consider these two scenarios as possible prototypes:

Tell me what you would do if you found $100,000.

Here's $100. Show me how you'd spend it.

The first approach can generate only conjecture in response, while the second can show a real result. A hundred dollars in hand isn't trivial. It feels real because it's not hypothetical and the scale is significant.

3 **Make it an experience, always.**

An experience offers a participant the chance to engage with a question or situation in a real way, through an activity of senses and emotions. This is one difference between making a prototype and conducting a survey or an interview. Make it a goal to always ask with an experience rather than just words.

Instead of asking a new college graduate, "What is most important in your life right now?" ask with an experience: spend $100 in a way that is important to your life right now. The experience can expand beyond an answer like "save for the future" and focus on real details, like *Where do I actually stash my savings?* or *Do I spend the money on gifts for friends? Maybe spend it on repairs to a bicycle for commuting to the new job?* An experience will always deliver useful information that a question alone can't cover.

You're ready to go! With clear questions, objectives, and mindsets, you're prepared to prototype. *Everything* else builds on these core components.

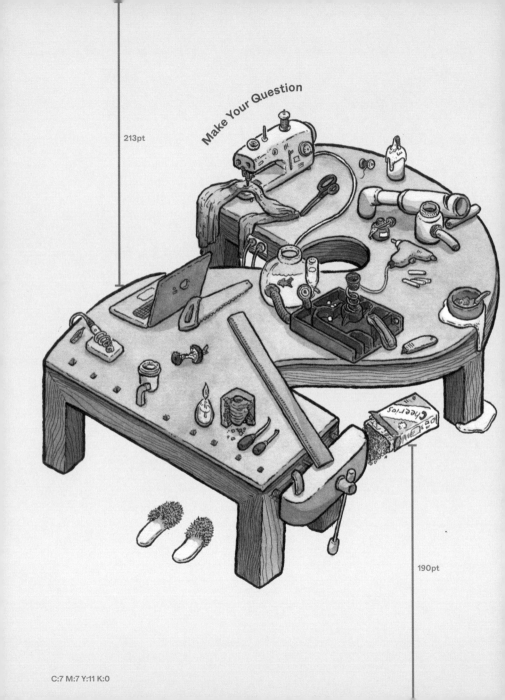

Make Your Question

213pt

190pt

C:7 M:7 Y:11 K:0

What Do I Need to Start?

Sanchez Semibold 60pt

The time to start making a prototype is right now. Unlike a product that is purportedly perfect before it hits the shelves, your prototype has to be only good enough to match what you want to learn at the moment. The best-built prototypes are measured by what you learn from them, not by how they look. That point of view will guide you in selecting the tools and materials you'll need to make a question into a prototype. This chapter will help you navigate the resources you'll need in order to begin.

Sanchez Semibold 9pt

Tools and Materials

The best prototyping tools are the tools that you actually use. This is insultingly simple and probably disappointing—especially since the tools you use most frequently don't always represent your (or their) best capabilities. But prototyping isn't an exercise for demonstrating the extent of your skills. It's an effort to put your skills to use most quickly and efficiently by always being prepared to build. That comes back to the best tools being the ones you can access and activate without any obstacles.

What tools have you deliberately placed around you to be able to make, embody, and prototype something right now? If you are sitting in a blank space or with empty pockets, this is a great time to adopt a new approach by outfitting yourself with resources: physical tools, digital tools, materials, and doodads that you can transform into something new.

Here's a list of tools and materials as you consider the resources surrounding you. It is up to you to determine whether this helps you feel perfectly prepared to prototype. Check off the items you have (or have access to). Cross out items you know you dislike. Add items you already use. Adjust accordingly to make this *your* list, please.

Pencils and pens
Black markers, fine and fat
Set of colored markers
Erasers
Ruler
Measuring tape

+

Compass
Protractor
Circle / shape templates
French curves
Long straight-edge
for cutting

+

Scissors
Hole punch
X-Acto knife
Box cutter
Cutting mat

+

Post-It type sticky notes
(square and rectangular in
different sizes)

8.5 × 11 / A4 copy paper
11 × 17 / A3 copy paper
Colored paper
Butcher paper
Kraft paper rolls
Tracing paper

+

Foam board (¼" thick and
½" thick)
Cardboard (bought big
or trimmed from
shipping boxes)
Poster board
Cardstock

+

Popsicle / craft sticks
Toothpicks
Zip ties
Pipe cleaners / chenille
twists
Wire ties
Wire
Paper clips
Binder clips
Thumb tacks
Rubber bands
Magnets

+

Straws (plastic / paper)
PVC pipe
Pipe connectors

+

Fabric sheets
Tarps
Plastic sheeting
Felt
Aluminum foil
Plastic wrap
Balloons
Modeling clay

+

Envelopes
Paper plates
Bowls (paper / plastic)
Tyvek-type envelopes
Bubble wrap
Needle and thread

+

Painters tape
Masking tape
Adhesive tape
Duct tape

Electrical tape (black
and colors)
Stickers (round dots / stars)

+

Staples
Stapler
Hot glue gun
Glue stick
All-purpose glue
(white glue)
Wood glue (yellow glue)
Super glue
Rubber cement
Spray adhesive

+

Legos
Lego gear sets
Wood and plastic blocks
Spools

+

Wind-up toy motors
Electronic prototyping
controllers (e.g., Arduino
and Raspberry Pi)
Soldering iron

Circuit components
Breadboards
Lightbulb(s)
LED strips
String lights with plug

+

Ink-jet / laser printer

+

Extension cords
Multi-outlets

+

Crosscut saw
Hacksaw

+

Tin snips / metal shears

+

Screwdrivers
Drill drivers
(battery operated)
Driver bit set

Drill bit set
Hammer

+

Quick clamps
C-clamps
Spring clamps (A-clamps)

+

Brads
Tacks
Nails
Screws

+

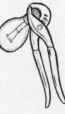

Tweezers
Channel-lock pliers
Needle-nose pliers
Adjustable pliers
Crescent wrench
Box wrenches
Allen or hex wrenches

+

Wood files
Metal files
Sandpaper
Rasp—for wood or foam

+

Router
Jigsaw
Circular saw

+

3-D printer
Sewing machine
Laminator
Vinyl cutter
Laser cutter

+

Computer
Mobile device
Digital camera
Drafting / graphics software
3-D modeling software
Portable projector

+

Plywood
Casters
Plastic crates

Build a Relationship with Your Resources

Starting with such a big list of tools and materials can feel prescriptive and overwhelming. Consider the resources you choose to use. Instead of starting with a premise of what is right or required, look for the tools and materials you feel most confident with. There's plenty of magic in simple tools and opportunity in the ordinary. Your work will reflect the way you interpret and use any item as a resource. This is a beautiful (and personal) part of prototyping the unknown. With this approach, you can feel confident authoring an approach of your own.

Think Inside and Outside the Box

When you approach your work with the goal of making do with what you have, you can shift from thinking *I must have this particular tool in order to connect these pieces* to focusing on the question *How can I connect these pieces?* or *Is there something ready-made I could use?* Having a vision for what you are trying to achieve with your prototype can be more important than limiting yourself to preconceived definitions of tools and materials.

Consider a cardboard box: it may be a good raw material for the cardboard alone. It could also be a tool or prop, as is. If your prototype calls for a container, problem solved. Likewise, if you are looking for a hinge mechanism, cut out the crease along an edge and you're ready to glue it in place somewhere else. Sparking an idea with a fire? Burn the box. In that quick consideration, you might discover

something new about the ideal list of tools and materials: your motivation with each item dictates a new way of being intentional about your work.

When you prototype, your own interpretation and imagination inform how you consider something as a tool or a material. For example, Toni Morrison kept her tools simple. The author and professor described her draft-writing tools in a 1993 interview for *The Paris Review:* "I'm not picky, but my preference is for yellow legal pads and a nice number two pencil." In someone else's hands, the same yellow legal pad that Morrison favored is also a really excellent material for simulating a digital app sequence—each page is another screen with a different navigation choice. There you go! Depending on the user and the intention, the same item could be a material, a tool, and a prototype experience all in one.

Organize Organically

Vinyl is back, and the return of record stores cues a new question: how do you arrange the goods? Some stores favor alphabetizing, while others curate by category or genre. Then there's the issue of sorting new versus used albums. It may be musical mayhem, but the intent in any case is worth stealing: be deliberate and organize your resources in a way that works for you.

Categorizing your resources is one way to match intent with an inventory. For example, consider the following categories as one way to organize that large list by *function* instead of by *ingredients*.

Structural items: PVC pipes, wood, craft sticks, clay, pipe cleaners

Cutting utensils: scissors, saws, box cutters, hole punches

Connecting utensils: stapler, painter's tape, glue, binder clips

Marking and measuring implements: markers, pens, and pencils; rulers, protractors

Pliable materials: rubber bands, modeling clay, aluminum foil, paper

Infrastructure and inspiration: boxes, decks of cards, stickers, balloons

It's an entirely different way to interpret and identify what you can do with what you have instead of placing a limit on your potential based on what you don't have. You'll still find gaps, but you might also see new opportunities with resources that cross categories. This step is worth exploring in order to move away from assumptions and artificial constraints.

Keep It Quick and Dirty

Match your resources to your confidence in the question you are asking. A low-fidelity or low-res prototype is intentionally a quickly assembled concept, created with nonprecious materials in order to explore an early concept, and nothing more. Hi-res prototypes take more time and ask more complicated questions. Since early questions are often in service of discovery, it is a good practice to match your materials and methods with quick and inexpensive work that you don't mind abandoning once the learning happens. As your confidence in a concept builds, based on what you've learned, you can also feel confident in dialing up your resources.

The tricky part of doing quick-and-dirty work is that your own skills can get in the way of making successful prototypes. Any expectation of your own expertise (ahem, ego) can crush your intention to start a less-than-perfect version of something—especially when you have the know-how to make perfect things. Perfectionism is problematic during the early stages of exploration. It takes practice and constant attention to match your work at the moment with the question of the moment. Try out this two-question gut check as part of your practice:

Is my work too high-resolution right now?

What's a "cardboard" version of this I could try first?

Another strategy for keeping yourself on track with low-fidelity prototypes is *diminishing your tool.* Designer and educator Charlotte Burgess-Auburn describes this approach as choosing a tool or technique that will keep your work consistent with the resolution of the question being asked. As an example, a digital animator choosing a diminished tool might pick pen and paper instead of a digital device and display to draw out storyboards. The resulting nonprecious paper panels can be shuffled around and marked up, unlike work that is polished for production. The output is just below what you might consider a final product. That imperfection is intentional, to invite feedback. Practice that principle: choose your tools at one or two levels of resolution *lower* than your final output in order to focus first on a question instead of fit and finish.

Space for Making

Tables, timing, training, technology—each has a place in a shop and is important to prototyping. The designation of a space as a specific place for making is well established with myriad names: studio, workshop, and atelier are just a few. Instead of looking for a defined place with the ideal resources for making something, build a habit of making wherever you may be. Prototype right where you are. In turn, see your own space as an ever-ready tool in and of itself, not just a place that holds tools. This is a way to make *making* a part of every activity in a way that is fundamentally different from confining creation to a certain time or room.

Outfit Yourself for Action

Your prototyping path will lead you to many places. Outfit yourself so that at any given moment you can get started with what you have and beg, borrow, or steal whatever else is around. Surfaces and storage set up the infrastructure for all your work. Experiment with configuring these resources in a way that works for you. Seriously: move things around.

Desks, tables, and floors are fine and familiar choices for horizontal work surfaces. Vertical surfaces like walls and windows are often overlooked as options, but they're frequently flat, clean, and available for creating and displaying visual work. They help you take action when a conventional choice won't do. Regardless of the option, keep your work surfaces clear and ready to go.

The goals of good storage are having a place for every tool or material and making sure everything is ready and available. Interacting with materials is both a great way to create casual inspiration and a reminder that you have ready resources. That easy access is also the gateway for the relentless creep of materials into your workspaces. So as you assemble an inspirational inventory, don't let it become clutter that slows down your work in progress.

Price never has to be a barrier here. Depending on the space you have, a killer configuration can come from a few plastic crates, some zip ties, a few boards, and some casters. Your intent can inform how you arrange your space with the quantity and configuration of resources you have. These ingredients work whether you are a designer or not, on your home turf or traveling abroad.

Here is a spectrum of outfitting examples with tools, equipment, and tactics to consider, wherever you may be, physically or professionally.

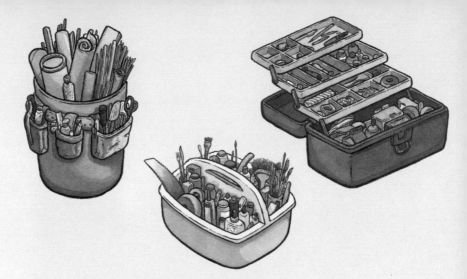

Personal Proto Kit

Assembling this mobile collection of small stuff is a huge step: it signals that wherever you are, you are equipped and ready to make. It is surface-agnostic: you can have it at your desk or take it to a room down the hall. Either way you won't go broke by having a couple of kits in different locations. The goods:

> Basic tools to help you visualize, such as pens, markers, and so on
>
> A select set of paper, like sketch books, copy paper, and sticky notes
>
> Some kinds of connectors, such as tape and a stapler
>
> Some oddball inspirational items, like pipe cleaners, a matchbox car, or some springs
>
> Few (if any) powered or accessory-dependent tools, like drills

The Mobile Rig

The mobile rig might move with you or deploy from a storage spot (such as in a closet or under a counter). A mobile station with containers for tools and materials is one of the highest impact assets that can help individuals and organizations transform existing "nonwork spaces" into prototyping shops. Construction *can* happen in a conference room.

Your rig does not have to look like it came from a dystopian future. Art carts, butcher blocks on casters, bathroom caddies, and old-school beverage busses can all do just as well as an industrial-strength rig.

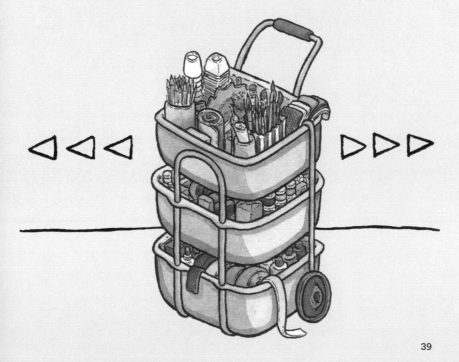

The Dedicated Workstation

Gather around the table! This configuration takes cues from professional kitchens and fabric shops that anchor activities around a large work surface. A prototyping workstation mirrors these myriad functions by supporting adaptability. This setup might match a large work surface with some version of a mobile rig: tools and resources that can move around easily. Because large surfaces can accommodate a lot of materials for making, over time they tend to accumulate leftovers. If you find you have access to more space, make it a point to create a cleanup protocol. Start and end with a clear workspace.

Studio or Workshop

This is the dream of any prototyper! A studio gives the obvious benefits of a controlled space, more surfaces for working, and increased capacity to support tools and resources. If you have a studio or are seeking one, set it up in a way that reduces barriers to getting started. Aim to find the fewest steps—mental and physical—needed to turn an idea in your head into a reality. This goal will help you decide whether something in your shop should stay or go. Keep reconfigurability as a top priority with your tools, work surfaces, and material storage. Even the biggest and best shops can get cluttered, regardless of size. There is an unfortunate parallel here to highway design—no matter how many lanes you build, traffic will always increase. When a tool or arrangement begins to accumulate dust, that is a signal to seriously consider whether it is keeping you active in your prototyping efforts.

Regardless of where *your* space falls on this range, keep watching for the ways that other places and organizations arrange their resources. Woodshops, bicycle workshops, and bakeries are just some of the spots that can inspire you with new behaviors and configurations.

Building Blocks for Prototyping

Design legend Bill Moggridge approached prototyping with a cheeky, two-question check: *Am I designing something new? Or am I designing a new version of something?* For example: *Am I seeking a new understanding of nutrition, or am I making it less messy to bring lunch to work?* "Designing something new" suggests that you are on a wholly original path with little precedent or reference. That is daunting, but it also suggests that you are not beholden to any particular answer or preexisting solution. You've got freedom! (And a lot to learn.) The other end of the spectrum—designing a new version of something—offers a quicker start and comes with constraints. You can work from state-of-the-art examples and current practices and products. This approach to prototyping comes from a designer but applies to anything, from planning a vacation to reconfiguring mass manufacturing.

Whether they're working on something unexplored or the next version of an existing concept, designers build from a stockpile of resources in addition to raw materials: parts and pieces, templates, and examples from previous work—their own and the work of others. They saturate their physical and digital workspaces with examples to inspire ideas and action more quickly than starting from scratch. Look at your own starting point—in your mind as well as the space around you—to take inventory of examples, artifacts, and inspirations you can turn into new ideas.

The following building blocks are stockpiled from some best practices for starting low-resolution prototypes. Used alone or in combination, each of these methods serves a single prototyping intent: to plausibly emulate *enough* of a situation to give someone a real experience. This is not an exhaustive collection. You might not find the right start here, but you might activate the memory of an analogous example you've encountered. It is almost guaranteed that you'll find a new way of doing something by seeing how someone else did it. Great! Capture that example and add it to your collection.

Contents

Start your set of Building Blocks with the following six examples.

Building Blocks

What It Is: No metaphor here; this Building Block is literal building blocks—physical objects that you can use to create form and function for an idea.

How You Can Use It:

Building blocks are placeholders with physical form—they can become as specific as need be or remain anonymous in acting out a scenario. They have structure, size, and shape, and with a bit of imagination or context can easily transform one thing into another. A cardboard box can become a podium, a refrigerator, or a placeholder for a supercomputer. You can use blocks to create settings and scenery to embody a new idea or set a context for a prototype.

Your blocks can take shape from stacked buckets, towered boxes, or aligned crates. Through their volume, quantity, and arrangement, the *size* of a prototype suddenly has significance. Will it *fit* over there? How can people get around it? Will it intimidate kids? Once an idea has size and function, people can start to really understand it without having to imagine or project.

→ A student uses large foam blocks to create an immersion room for classmates. This not-at-all-childish approach makes impromptu architecture possible and useful. Building blocks change the scale of an experience from hand-held or hypothetical to full-sized for human engagement.

↑ The lead curator for the San Francisco Museum of Modern Art (SFMoMA) uses the concept of building blocks ("maquettes" in museum-speak) to represent each piece of art in the museum's holdings. The blocks each have just enough look-and-feel to be representative, but they function collectively as props for prototyping the possibilities for new exhibit configurations. Collaborators can react and reconfigure the pieces, turning feedback into an actual demonstration instead of a description.

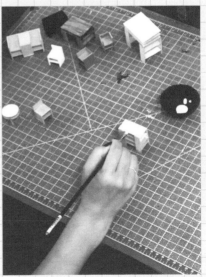

47

Parts and Pieces with Functions

What It Is: A pile of parts and pieces (physical and digital) with existing functions that you can mash together to accelerate your prototyping work.

How You Can Use It: You can leverage the function of existing bits and bobs to make something new or to at least avoid a time sink of having to create mechanisms anew. Researchers in human computer interaction at Stanford call this "opportunistic design," a common practice among toy designers. It's not just a practice of saving time by using existing parts; it's also an act of seeking inspiration from the look, feel, and function of the parts around you. A box full of wind-up toys and pinwheels sitting at your station might inspire you to prototype a gear-driven window shade *and* provide some of the parts to get started.

Parts and pieces can also include digital tools like functional bricks of computer code or plug-and-play digital devices (microprocessors with functional parts, like the tiny Raspberry Pi boards or Arduino computers). Functions within existing apps can be raw materials for prototypes that use the tools. However, don't depend on apps as overall answers—use a survey, share an image, or crowdsource feedback using the functionality as the off-the-shelf offering.

← Legendary musician and producer Money Mark continually experiments with new sounds by combining the functions—beeps and motions—of all kinds of things: toys, power tools, batteries, wires, hoses, and horns. All are bits he keeps around to make new noises.

→ Lonesoulsurfer is an inventor and explorer who constantly adapts components from discarded devices into new uses. In this case, a vintage bike lamp with a burnt-out bulb shed light on the option of adding an LED. That all combined with a discarded drum stand and—BOOM!— it's a bike lamp light with functionality, inspired by and accelerated into fruition from bits of things within reach.

Intentional Blanks

What It Is: Any kind of ready-to-go template—print or graphic—with blank spaces to be filled in following a prototyping prompt.

How You Can Use It:

Intentional blanks provide an immediate infrastructure of form and flow to capture a prototype idea. Blanks provide just enough structure to get started. The function follows the formula from the Mad Libs game, using a story full of blank spaces that someone can fill in for fun.

The quintessential visual blank is a storyboard. Storyboards show a sequence of events and the flow of interactions. The film and animation industries use this straightforward tool to match a visual scene with a note about the action taking place in each frame. Being able to shuffle, add, and subtract scenes allows everyone to understand, align, and adjust content before anything gets built or filmed. This utility makes storyboards a go-to tool for prototyping almost any experience.

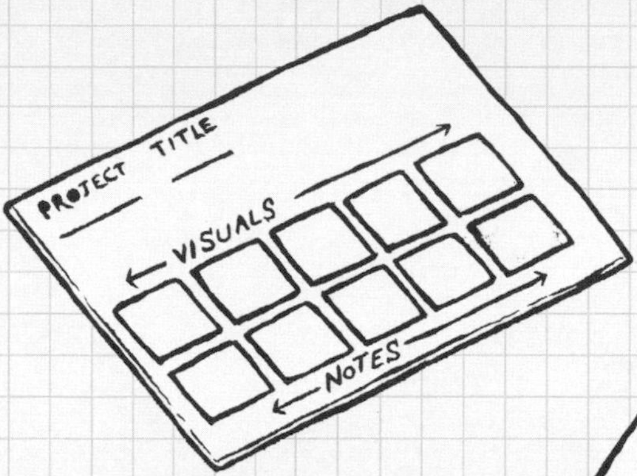

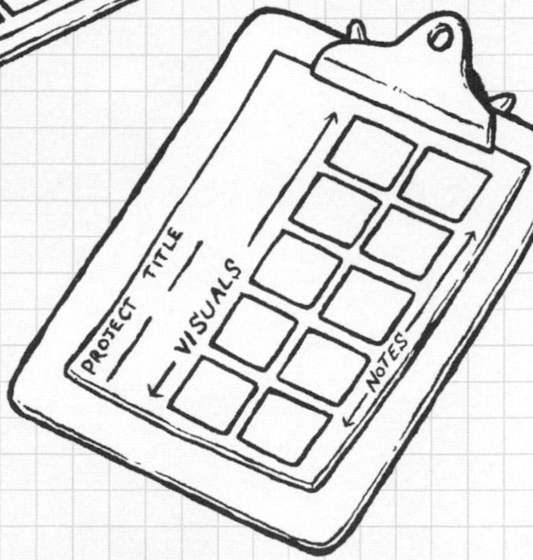

↑ Consider the simple five-step template shown here. With any number of boxes, an orientation for flow, and some simple prompts for title, description, and a sketch, you have the basis for a prototype experience that will work the same way whether you create and share a digital template or print out a stack of worksheets.

BB_04: BMP

Behavior Maps

What It Is: A fill-in-the-blank mapping space paired with basic prompts for visualizing a flow, interaction, or description.

How You Can Use It:

Graphic maps serve as an effective tool for connecting abstract concepts to a physical and interactive experience. You can map an activity, a location, or a concept. Maps make a great start to a conversation with participants; they are also excellent artifacts to collect for reference later in the process of your work.

Maps help make abstract concepts more tactile, visible, and (hopefully) understandable. With text alone you might spend a lot of time reading between the lines, guessing at the meaning of what is *not* written. With a map you can actually see the interstitial spaces—gaps between things—and focus on understanding connections.

A mapping activity can start simply and add complexity to reveal and combine layers of information. Start with a simple prompt: draw a map of your day. Then try something more complex, depending on your objective; say, create a map of places where you feel safe in your community. The result is itself a record that may offer more information than a verbal or text-based response.

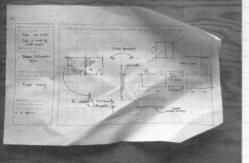

A typical map might look like a grid or graph paper template along with a prompt asking someone to map out a behavior. The view can be bird's eye (from above) or an elevation (like a cross-section). Your template can be as simple as a portion of a printable sheet with grid or graph lines along with some prompts at the side. Preprinted prompts next to gridlines can help guide people in the moment, as shown with this prototype of a new office furniture layout.

→ Design educator Carissa Carter used a set of five written prompts asking people around the world to draw freeform maps of how they understand how water gets to their homes. Their responses ranged from hand-drawn to digital diagrams of all different shapes and annotation styles.

WATER TREATMENT PLANT

MY HOUSE

AQUIFER

San Diego, California, U.S.A.
23 years old
I am a young interneter.
I am an expert in delicious snacks

← Maps can also be physical and interactive experiences, as is the case with the classic example of sand maps used by the military to quickly demonstrate operations and allow people to physically engage parts and pieces to ask questions.

Digital Templates in 2-D and 3-D

What It Is: A "clean slate" digital workspace tuned with a few details or tools in place to support visualizing right away each time you start a new project. (For a cooking demonstration, this would be a digital version of a kitchen prepped with clean counters, pots and pans out, and veggies already chopped.)

How You Can Use It:

Professionals who work with drafting (CAD) and modeling (CAM) software create templates that are ready to go when new two-dimensional and three-dimensional projects come along. Every new project varies, but drafters set themselves up with preset features and character-istics to save time translating concepts into visualizations as prototypes. This includes prese-lecting fonts for typing, certain viewpoints to start drawing, and varieties of materials and elements that often pop up in products. Some designers (and some programs) have default shapes already in place.

Presentation software is a surprisingly excellent tool for creating visual prototypes. Skip the "slide deck" use case and reframe boardroom standards like PowerPoint and Keynote as quick and customizable graph-ics tools. To start, abandon the default gradient themes and clip-art clutter to create a blank template slide as a big work space—set up some guidelines as a grid, pick your fonts, and choose some colors. Each of these details takes time when you're in the moment, so do it once and save it for later.

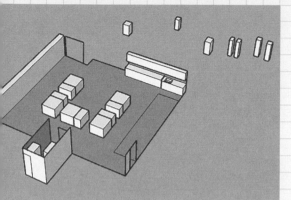

← Joe Romano is a middle school teacher who used SketchUp—an easy-entry, 3-D drawing package—to prototype a new makerspace over a summer break before building anything. Romano used simple, blocky shapes to shuffle around to consider what to buy, what to build, and how to fit it all together. He now uses that digital template to regularly reimagine new options for the room setup.

Quick One-Clicks

What It Is: Whether web, app, mobile, desktop, cloud, or otherwise, these are existing digital products or platforms you can turn into an immediately engageable part of a prototype.

How You Can Use It: Each digital product is the quickest example to access a function you might find useful for the moment—an ingredient to an experience instead of a final version or format. An example of a quick one-click is any app with built-in functionality that would allow you to add a decision-making step into the sequence of an experience. That reaction could take shape any number of ways depending on the tool you use—vote, like, post, share, poll, draw, rearrange, etc. One-clicks don't have to represent how your work will ultimately look, feel, or operate.

Ask yourself, "What's a ready-to-go version of this that I could use?" This is a moving inventory of options! As you finish this sentence, an existing example will have gone out of business and two others will have emerged. Focus on the function itself as you continually update your options. Set some constraints like the following to build out your collection of one-click "go-to" tools:

+ Posting video and digital content so someone else can interact

+ Setting up a financial transaction to simulate a business or campaign

+ Getting feedback, such as through yes/no responses, voting, or comments

+ Collaborating on a shared artifact (such as a calendar or map)

Motivated by large numbers of people dying in isolation during the COVID-19 pandemic, a social-design group called the Emergency Design Collective explored how to start end-of-life conversations with loved ones before illness strikes. They created prototypes using the record-and-share video function in the existing Marco Polo mobile app to explore the limits of conversations that close friends have about end-of-life planning. The app wasn't intended as part of a solution but offered a feature that worked well as a tool to elicit specific behaviors.

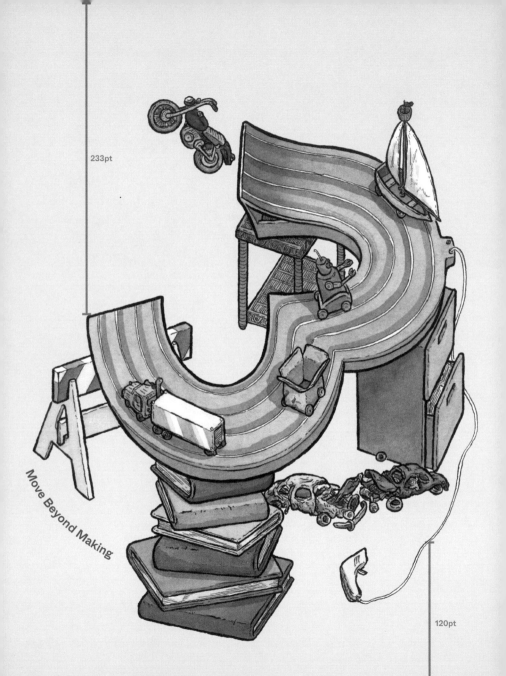

233pt

Move Beyond Making

120pt

C:7 M:7 Y:11 K:0

What Should I Do Now?

There is a moment in prototyping when you move from maker to moderator and shift from being the author of an idea to an observer of action. This is a letting-go moment—letting go of something that you made. (Cue the danger.) It is an understatement to say that it is hard to let go of your work, but it is a requirement. Making this transition successfully works best when you celebrate your skills and then step away from what you've made to see how it plays out in an experience. This chapter explores how to move from what you've made toward making the best out of what you witness. It's a fresh take on seeing how your work can and will take on a new shape.

Celebrate the Power and Joy of Making

It feels great to build something! Early work often reflects a lack of skill or a low-res approach—the fit and finish are usually a little shabby. You might feel sheepish about the quality but still excited about the effort. That excitement connects to important topics: a maker's motivations and what it means to do good work. Why do people make things, and what does making mean to them? *What does your work mean to you?*

Let's look at Girls Garage to understand this ethos. Emily Pilloton-Lam is an architect, educator, and activist. She founded Girls Garage as an organization to give young girls the tools they need to build anything. In *Girls Garage* (the book, not the garage), Pilloton-Lam describes a pivotal moment in her own history of making:

> *In graduate school in Chicago, I walked into the fabrication shop and said, 'Teach me how to weld.' I learned how to braze and MIG weld in a matter of days—and haven't stopped since. Fusing metal felt superhuman and opened up a whole new world of possible ideas to build. Welding taught me (literally and metaphorically) how to bring the fire to my work.*

Pilloton-Lam declares, "Your identity as a builder matters. Who you are is not separate from what you build or why. . . . Bring your heart and your story to what you create, and scream who you are through your tools."

When you start to build something, you may actually discover a new version of yourself that you never knew existed. It's critical to understand *what* you build and *why,* because your identity as a builder matters. That perspective applies to prototypes, not just perfect products. For many people, the first act of making something is electric, nearly intoxicating in its appeal. The act and recognition of "I made this from nothing" is a profound step in becoming a confident person who feels agency to do it again—and again. The challenge comes in seeing yourself as a person capable of making as a practice rather than someone who made that one thing, that one time.

It's easy to judge yourself based on what you make, and often the things you build are measured by appearance: If it looks good, *you* are good. However, when it comes to making prototypes, the motivations behind how and why you make something are more difficult to evaluate. As we know, the best prototypes often don't need to be the best built. This challenges a convention that aesthetics alone determines worth. The worth of your creations extends beyond appearance into experience. Moving forward confidently with an understanding of how and why you did your work is one of the most celebratory moments of making . . . anything.

It is important, however, to note the subtle and substantial tension between being a skilled prototyper and a skilled craftsperson. The prototyper must let go of their crafted work, knowing that it is disposable by definition, in service of learning what must come next. The craftsperson, by contrast, can approach their work with the intent of output as a treasure—embodying the extent of skill in making an object. The prototyper and craftsperson are not mutually exclusive, but their objectives often are. When you are learning a new skill, your output is imperfect, becoming better with mastery. When you are prototyping, your "products" are deliberately imperfect because they are interim tools for learning about other things. It helps to understand the role of each creation or output so that you can reflect and move beyond what you made.

Steady Yourself for Separation Anxiety

Surrendering your work is the first step toward learning from it, marking a shift from being a creator of a thing to a curator of an experience. Turning a trophy into trash does not feel good (and that is only a slightly melodramatic description of making and breaking a prototype). Here's a lesson to lessen the impact of this reality: designate a deliberate moment to mark letting go of this stage of your work.

Verena Paepcke-Hjeltness is an educator and designer who helps students learn the skills of turning ideas into reality, through sketching, fabrication, and manufacturing. Separating early work from final outcomes is a lesson that she teaches through an exercise in hand rendering—the practice of illustrating high-fidelity, realistic product graphics by hand. As part of a lengthy product development project, students are required to create renderings of their early concepts. At the end of a couple weeks of this work, and immediately following the group presentation of these drawings, Paepcke-Hjeltness requires her students as a group to tear up their final renderings. Tears.

We can learn from Paepcke-Hjeltness's observations of this painful step:

> *The idea of tearing up the best sketch is not so much about not falling in love with that idea. It is geared*

toward not treating the sketch as a final outcome and instead seeing it as the vehicle to get to the final solution. The students often thought the sketch was the outcome, instead of treating it as a means to communicate the final solution."

Erica Estrada-Liou, a mechanical engineer and educator, teaches a complementary technique to avoid becoming overprotective of prototypes and feeling the trauma of letting them go. She describes this approach as "prototyping to invalidate." It's a mindset with which a prototyper looks for, and hopes for, ways that their prototypes don't work. Seeking to invalidate focuses attention on outcomes—lessons that emerge from experiences—rather than on the actual objects. This focus can come in the form of a question, when you or someone else starts asking, "What's missing here?" Even better is the reaction, "This is terrible. What this really should be is _____!"*

Prototyping to invalidate sets up a proactive detachment from the thing to create space for discovery. Once you've celebrated your work and set it free, it is much easier to learn from it instead of feeling obligated to sell or defend it.

Deliver the Experience

While a single objective from a prototyping experience is to learn, there is no single formula for designing the best actual experience. All of the steps you've taken—identifying your intent and objective, using low-resolution materials to start, working quickly from previous examples and inspiration—set you up to let go and let learning lead your work. But what does a prototype experience look like in real life?

During the late 2000s in San Francisco, several different organizations started experimenting with new ways for residents to safely get around the city. The experiences focused on the escalation of dangerous interactions between bicyclists and car drivers and more specifically the ways that cars as objects were disproportionately impacting people on the street—the cyclists and pedestrians. While none of the groups called these interventions "prototypes," each instance immediately fit the objectives of prototyping to explore, prototyping to provoke, and prototyping to understand. They combined big concepts and low-resolution examples into experiences to learn about the potential outcomes—that's a prototype!

The San Francisco Metropolitan Transformation Agency (SFMTrA) created a series of provocations using physical dividers along critical commuter corridors—streets that either saw a lot of bicycle traffic, had high vehicle counts but no separate bicycle lanes, or had frequent collisions. In

some cases, these physical dividers transformed car lanes into bicycle lanes. In other situations, the separations augmented the existing painted-only separations with physical structures (called "soft barriers") or built on existing barriers.

In another series of experiences, People Protected, founded by Maureen Perisco and Matt Brezina, staged stand-in experiences in which people lined up in streets along painted bicycle lane boundaries or along street lanes where such boundaries didn't exist. People standing hand in hand formed three-dimensional barriers with their bodies between car and bike lanes. These temporary boundaries changed the behaviors of drivers and cyclists along those streets, illuminating many issues: the absurdity of humans forming physical boundaries for cars; the immense scale difference between a car and a bicycle; and the threat and potential dangers to human life and safety in traveling along unprotected lanes. The reality of people standing in the street as a physical barrier seems implausible as any kind of long-term solution, which is exactly the point—and a benefit of this kind of making.

Both sets of prototypes resembled "looks like" and "works like" levels of resolution. They elicited actual behaviors in people who were otherwise going about their real-life routines. These experiences were provocative by nature but functionally different from an equivalent protest, speech, or presentation. By being physical and experiential, they moved beyond conversations and thoughts about policy to actual changes in policy.

These examples demonstrate how questions can be explored and embodied through prototypes. How are public streets used? How might streets be divided, shared, or separated for different modes of transportation? What does it mean to prioritize bicycle traffic? How can perceived dangers be visualized for a shared understanding? What does it look like to implement some "first draft" solutions? What can we learn from low-resolution versions of barriers, visual indicators, rearrangement of patterns? After successful explorations, what would the next-step versions be? What do we see not working with

these quick installations, and what would be the next iteration? Every "built" element could easily have been much
higher in resolution—bigger, stronger, more durable—but
the context of the exploration was not at that level, yet.

We can pick out the familiar principles from these examples and see how they can guide your own decisions:

> Abandoning the burden of perfectionism and using
> only what is needed helps make the outcomes
> clearer.
>
> Creating an immersive context with details that
> feel real leads to authentic reactions from people,
> instead of pretend or projected answers.
>
> Allowing people to engage with and, in some cases,
> change the details in front of them can inform
> the questions you are posing and illuminate new
> questions you haven't yet considered.

Each of these elements is a helpful step in turning anything that you have made into an evaluative experience
instead of an object on a shelf.

Prototype from Precedent

Stockpiling experience examples, like the ones just presented, offers the same benefit as gathering building blocks did in chapter 2. These examples, whether devised by you or someone else, are perfect for adapting for future use. Recasting concepts in a new way can feel a bit odd at first, but it's not a frivolous effort. You can approach previous prototype experiences with the same calculation as a lawyer seeking legal precedents to prepare for a case. While details might differ, there is something to be learned from previous situations that you can borrow or bend into a new way forward.

Stewart Brand, a do-it-yourself pioneer and founder of *The Whole Earth Catalog,* describes an architectural design principle called "adaptive reuse." It suggests that the built environment, consisting of structures of all kinds, experiences different lives based on the circumstances of the day. What was once a hospital may turn into a luxury hotel. A warehouse may transform into a high school; a main street into a farmers' market. You can adapt this circular behavior and its intent: collect experiences to reuse as raw materials for building out new ideas and opportunities.

The following Experience Catalog features a few best practices for creating prototype experiences. These examples serve a single intent: to plausibly emulate *enough* of a situation to help someone experience and respond to your prototype. Adapt anything to fit your current goals. Keep noticing and adding new methods of making to your personal catalog.

Contents

Build out your personal Experience Catalog with the following six examples.

EC_01: NBH

The No-Build Hack

The Use: Improvise as a way to understand an early concept or motivation. No-build hacks actively ignore fancy technology in favor of simply setting a context.

The Experience: No-build hacks are cobbled together with anything you have at hand. The goal is to create a context with the bare minimum you need to set the scene for a play. These prototypes often have some kind of tactile or sensory engagement. Your participants don't just watch; they do or react to something. This may involve taking on a new posture—standing up, sitting down, or otherwise taking on a new physical position to "enter" the prototype. Include anything that helps participants feel the essence of your experience, but don't fret over the functionality and infrastructure you'd expect (and have to invent) for a real-life solution. Rather than fiddling with design details, place the focus on noticing emergent behaviors. Simply put, gather together what you can to simulate an exploratory experience instead of a single solution.

Pros / Cons: Hacked-together experiences are simple and effective when they are distilled to the essence. A few details go a long way. All of the technological shortcomings make the initial prototypes implausible for understanding mechanical and functional details later in a process.

↑ A group of prototypers turned some basic furniture and piles of paper into an off-road vehicle to emulate a new tourism concept. The prototype featured a banquet table covered with sheets of paper and a chair placed atop the table. This hacked-together configuration simulated an AI-directed vehicle intended to help people explore new adventures.

To start the experience, participants "climbed into the Jeep," getting up onto the table to sit in the driver's seat. The prototypers then used paper displays of adventure options to understand how people might make decisions on their own or with the help of the AI vehicle system. The objectives were not to create the best (or even a plausible) interface or the most efficient vehicle. The intent was to understand how people might navigate choices if such a concept existed.

Volume (Speaks Volumes)

The Use: Volumetric and full-scale physical experiences to illuminate details easily missed in miniatures or models.

The Experience: A volumetric experience uses materials to create large-scale effects that might not be understood from a model or a drawing. Reactions like "I don't know how to build a wall" or "It will take a lot of time and materials to set up something like that" are legitimate mental obstacles to simulating a setting bigger than a person. The classic example of collecting large appliance boxes from home centers is an easy way to get large-volume building blocks. Foam or cardboard panels come in large standard sizes and can be repeatedly used and reconfigured. Rolls of paper or construction sheathing make for lightning-fast implementation of walls or barriers. PVC pipes and foam pool noodles are handy tools to create volumetric infrastructure without having to construct things in a conventional way.

Pros / Cons: A full-scale experience delivers a full-scale understanding. Big (and complex) results can come from simple, easily accessible materials that can quickly come together. Volumetric materials require some storage space: cardboard boxes and foam panels take up room. Having large-format materials on hand requires foresight, but rolls of paper, plastic sheathing, and masking tape are easily stored once you know that you'll need them.

↑ To explore future possibilities for their teaching and learning spaces, elementary school teachers in East Palo Alto prototyped classroom configurations and architectural details before a new school was built. An overhead grid of string suspended large paper panels that simulated movable wall partitions. Teachers and students used and modified these prototypes during normal class activities to experience how this type of infrastructure might (or might not) work for their needs. This bare-bones setup was a full-scale simulation of something that didn't yet exist, with novelties and nuances that became clear only once tested. This kind of makeshift reality can inform designs now without having to wait months or years for a first exposure to what will already be a final design.

Triage the Technology

The Use: Focusing on one technical detail at a time in order to advance to the next when exploring unknown technologies or complex functional systems.

The Experience: These experiences are most often used to test a function early on so you can move on to the next step. Focus on a single feature you are trying to test, and match it with the best technology you have at hand. After you have that figured out, move on to the next feature and do it again. Let that process guide your technology options for the moment, instead of freaking out about the final functionality. This "works like" prototype doesn't have to be pretty; it just has to function. Don't get caught up on the details you *might* need to deal with down the road. Right now, you only need to make sure the first thing works.

Pros / Cons: The challenge of making something work leads to a feeling of accomplishment when it does, and then that thing starts to feel like a finished product. The benefits of figuring out whether something will actually work take prototyping beyond pretend into a beautiful reality. The drawback is that functional prototypes are still learning tools, so it's important to keep further goals in mind but off the table. It is easy to get stuck in the weeds with a functional prototype.

↑ The CompactCath team designs urinary incontinence devices for people who require the daily use of catheters that they have to administer themselves. These products were never conceived to be socially convenient or discreet; their use is an awkward and intimate endeavor. From the start, the team faced the big challenge of *medical* design, asking, "How do we test this with *people*?" It's precisely the sort of situation that seems impossible for prototyping with low-resolution materials and imperfect early concepts.

When the team began, their final product wasn't obvious or even understood. They advanced by exploring individual elements one at a time. Many of these elements didn't even require access to people. They experimented with fluid mechanics by using straws, tubing, and existing products to emulate new catheter functions, shifting the form factor from long and narrow to coiled and collapsible. That led them to explore watertight materials and durability during daily carry. They tested interim concepts using anatomical models, before needing to practice with people. It was an incremental approach, breaking down each bit and matching it with a technical test appropriate at the moment.

Gamify It

The Use: Using the appeal and function of a game to create an engaging experience to explore a solution or better understand a behavior.

The Experience: The fundamental appeal of games makes them useful for prototyping experiences. Pay attention to what makes games work: incentive, competition, collaboration, discovery, and fun. You can create a goal or a sequence that directly explores a question you have with your prototype. For example: how would someone react if they found a lost dog? Make that the basis for a game! Most any topic can be gamified. Interaction is an important part of the experience, whether you're working physically or digitally. Take cues from board games with parts and pieces that people can control, and then see what happens when they do.

Pros / Cons: Games can translate any kind of concept into an experience. They communicate a fun and positive experience, which is often the opposite feeling someone expects from, say, a survey. That helps the person running the experience feel less on the hook to ask the right questions and get everything perfect; people like to play games, so you won't have to persuade them to participate. Games require playful effort and constraints, usually depending on multiple players and/or a set of rules.

← A team of students in Tokyo followed their curiosity about a theme they discovered doing fieldwork: living in a large city can be lonely, particularly for single people, regardless of age. The team framed their exploration with the question: how can we make local blocks less lonely? To prototype, they moved from a knee-jerk solution of an app into a board game–style experience to understand how and when people could interact in public more frequently, but without feeling self-conscious about it. The game included several prompts for people to use in order to make decisions about their daily behaviors. Crossing paths on the board mirrored strangers meeting for the first time.

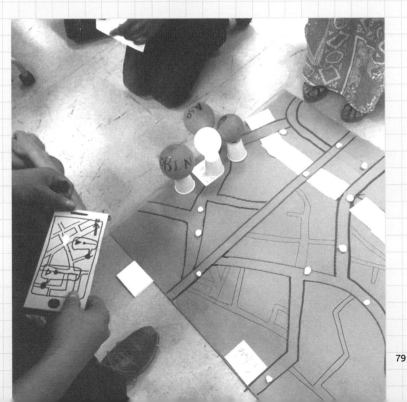

Pop-up Prototype

The Use: Create temporary experiences with a high-contrast context by using existing infrastructure or adding unique elements to an environment.

The Experience: Pop-up prototypes respond to a space and initiate a new behavior by using what is in place in a new way or adding new functional elements to facilitate the experience. This approach leverages the magic of a black box theater: an ambiguous stage that can be shaped in multiple different ways with minimal props and effects. The goal is to create a full-scale, real-life experience on a bounded stage where only key elements exist. Focus on methods that create immersion in the experience, without full-blown scenery. Crisp details and distilled props define the context. Those details might include directions for participation or an objective for a participant to follow. Consider the existing norms—the protocols, rules, regulations—to help make a prototype align with or deviate from expectations people might have as they engage.

Pros / Cons: Pop-up experiences are memorable because they are immersive and often stand in contrast to an existing situation. Success comes with planning the orchestration; you need to have control over a space to do it. Contexts that are familiar bring a lot of existing assumptions, so you must pay attention to trying something new in a context that already feels familiar. Distilling an experience to the minimal set of details can be a challenge the first time you try it.

↑ Blaine Merker and John Bela are designers and architects who focus on how people interact with their cities. In 2005 they started experimenting with popping up public parks within the boundaries and rules of metered street parking. Small grassy areas with seating and atmosphere just like a real park fit within the footprint of a parking space. As parking meters expired, the participants added more coins to continue occupying the area.

This experimentation inspired a new way of approaching how people can engage with public spaces. The example spread to cities internationally, motivating adaptations of this parklet to other small spaces to support dining, gathering, and recreation. Parklets, when viewed as temporary civic installations, have become a primary prototyping platform for auditioning new relationships and behaviors among the public, businesses, and government—informing new norms and allowing for pure experimentation.

Behavior by Boundaries

The Use: Cue behaviors and signal different ways to engage using visual or lightweight physical boundaries.

The Experience: Defining behaviors with visual cues is a powerful prototyping tool. Visual or otherwise impermanent boundaries show up everywhere in our daily lives—traffic lane stripes, train station queues, sports courts. You can use any variety of boundaries to establish behaviors that you would otherwise have to explain or demonstrate. Why tell someone to form a line when you can model it with a stripe on the floor? Likewise, you can elicit behaviors by deliberately omitting a boundary. How do people react when there is no guidance from below? Also consider this: lines and boundaries in physical spaces translate to boundaries on a page or in a set of instructions. Space designers and graphic designers use boundaries in a similar way.

Pros / Cons: Visual boundaries are highly effective for the effort. They require only simple materials to start and often can be removed instantly. Lightweight boundaries offer very little in the way of actual protection or structure; a bike lane is a covenant not a construction. Long-term implementation or robust performance requires more effort. Barriers and boundaries aren't always applicable in nonspatial experiences.

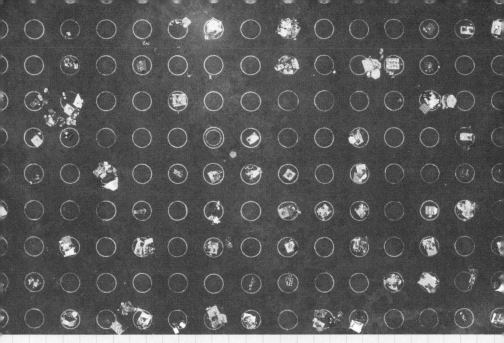

↑ Trying to squelch the early spread of the COVID-19 virus, cities everywhere experimented with different techniques to cue safe ways that people could gather in outdoor and indoor spaces. The City of San Francisco and its Park and Recreation Department adapted their field lining tools to paint pods in parks. These physical circles cued people to sit within the boundaries of their social circles to be safe. This effort to "try a possibility" allowed the city to observe actual public interactions without needing to build or know a structural solution based on conjecture instead of real behaviors.

Develop Your Own Experience

88pt

177pt

C:7 M:7 Y:11 K:0

How Should I Test This?

Sanchez Semibold 60pt

The way you create a prototype experience rests on the explicit ask: "How should I test this?" The complement to this question is "How should I show up in order to evaluate this experience?" That is, what is your role once the prototype is under way? Evaluating your prototype means focusing on your own behaviors as much as it does on creating a good prototype from the start. This may seem like a lot to juggle, but any work in service of one objective actually helps with both. This chapter explores developing your own skills for designing experiences and evaluating them.

Sanchez Semibold 9pt

C:100 M:40 Y:0 K:20

Warm Up to Being a Host

As the creator of a prototype, you naturally qualify to be the host of your prototype experience. What should your objectives be as the host? Let's look to the dinner party for inspiration. In her essay, "The Art of the Dinner Party," New York City–based chef and restaurateur Gabrielle Hamilton illuminates a near-perfect parallel of dinner party and prototype goals:

> To me it has always been clear that a dinner party is about what is said, not what is eaten. There would always be wine and salad and bread and stew; chocolate and fruit and nuts and sparkling cold duck. But those were just the props—the conduits for funny and real and meaningful conversation; the set pieces of a lively, engaged, lingering old-school dinner party.

Of course, a dinner depends on *the dinner*—the fundamental food to be eaten. There is value and craft embedded in the eats, but they're a vehicle for something more. Hamilton suggests that the value of the event emerges from the experience, not just assembling and serving the ingredients. The host, whether a chef or not, facilitates with a set of sometimes-hidden skills beyond perfect meal preparation: listening, observation, improvisation, and collaboration.

As a host, you face similar questions to those of someone learning from a prototype. What is the invitation you offer?

Are you prepared to present options? Are you ready to listen? Are you ready to ask about someone else? Are you able to look past what you've made to find meaning from someone else's interpretation? Are you able to adapt in the moment?

Responding with a host's posture of service—offering adaptability and alternatives—is something we all know how to do but might not think to put into practice when it comes time to prototyping. This is a critical posture for remaining objective and side-stepping any offense you might take from someone not liking your work. As a host, you wouldn't tell a guest that they *do* in fact enjoy eating a meal they are allergic to or that their soup is piping hot even though the guest says it's tepid. These examples may seem silly, but that is almost the exact instinct people have when faced with others evaluating their work. It's a natural defense, but it's an obstacle to the goals of throwing a good party and creating a successful experience. Success through sharing your prototypes requires a focus on your own behaviors as much as it does on creating good proto-types from the start.

Double-Check: Are You Serving Up an Experience or Showing Off an Artifact?

Are you really ready? We can gut check the difference by looking at one challenge that a group of Carnegie Mellon students faced: redesigning a fire extinguisher. The students took on this challenge by first thinking *I'm going to make a better fire extinguisher* and then asking *What do I think could be better?* Of course, they weren't focusing on themselves as the only users. Fire extinguishers are for everybody, and that's where the students started: asking people other than themselves.

During an exploratory experience, students asked a person to pick up a familiar fire extinguisher and put out a small fire. In setting up this scenario, they shifted their focus from the thing itself to how it gets used. Doing so, they learned that fire extinguishers actually aren't that familiar to most folks. Many people have never used them and fumble while trying to do so in the heat of the moment. From direct observation, the students saw that the features and functions that make an extinguisher seem like the best product on the shelf were some of the exact details that were ignored when it came to actual use. That discovery shifted the students' trajectory from a device-driven output to behavior-based options. To inform new possibilities, they delineated the difference between telling

someone how they should theoretically act versus drawing inspiration from a real reaction.

The approach leading to this significant reframing is one we can celebrate—and steal! *Let's find opportunities from behaviors instead of first focusing on features.* Make sure that whatever you have made and are sharing, showing, or asking is paired with an experience that allows behaviors to emerge.

Identify (with) Your Authentic Audience

It's a common concept to test an idea *on* someone, saying, "I tested this prototype on a bunch of people, and here is what I learned." As you encounter this expression in your own activities, shift that thinking, not just the phrasing. The way to move forward is designing *with* someone and prototyping an experience *with* someone or *with* an audience.

By bringing something to fruition—the fruit of prototyping!—you become responsible for connections between that work and the people it affects. Those connections start when you seek feedback, and they build as your work extends beyond yourself into someone else's life. As that happens, it's important to acknowledge, invite, and activate the expertise of people in their own experiences. When you find yourself doing work for an audience other than yourself, consider this question: how are you making space for them to contribute and collaborate with you?

Meeting new people *where they are* is an amazing part of prototyping that moves beyond seeing only yourself in your work. Assessing your role with an audience before conducting any work is a fundamental part of the Liberatory Design process, which features an equity-first practice. Created by a team from

the National Equity Project and the Stanford d.school, this intent applies here in order to ensure that prototypes as exploration do not become tools for exploitation. This includes approaching any stage of your work with a suite of dynamic mindsets that balance how you are thinking and acting with the life situations of other contributors, such as interview participants, a design audience, and collaborators.

Just as you've considered the work you hope to share, consider the steps necessary for aligning yourself with an audience you hope to understand. Building on Liberatory Design practices, you can use the following prompts to prepare and support your connection with others:

Reflect on your role in this situation.

Reflect on the role of someone you are engaging.

Open up this reflection to conversation so that everyone can express their understanding.

Ask yourself and adjust accordingly:

Am I exerting influence knowingly or unknowingly?

Am I approaching from an extractive position or a collaborative position? That is, am I taking from them—whether that is time, resources, or the value of their life experience?

Am I listening for and acknowledging complexities in someone else's life that may not fit a model I have in mind?

Set Your Scene Strategically

The space for experiencing a prototype should be as considered as the space for making it. Context counts, and a fruitful experience depends on a sprinkle of stagecraft in preparation. Set up your scenario to support yourself, your work, and your audience.

Consider any unintentional barriers to participation with your prototype. Is this model too delicate to touch with clumsy hands? For digital experiences, do those in your audience have to create an account to engage with your concept? Does a very long explanation get in the way of someone's diving into what you have in mind? Your ability to learn from prototypes is directly connected to how easy or difficult it is for others to engage them. Whatever you make, build in a low barrier.

Start every experience by helping your audience understand the context so they are ready for what's to come (unless surprise is an element you are excited to explore). Setting the stage is a delicate balance of engaging people with respect without over-explaining events to the point of dulling the encounter.

Lisa Kay Solomon is an expert in designing strategic conversations—setting up and diagnosing all the details necessary for people to come together for successful communication. She explains that people are "wired for

certainty." That is, people engage in familiar circumstances with some anticipation of certainty in the outcome. For example, people operate with expectations like *I'm going to a meeting to talk about X,* or *At the end of this event, I will have an outcome.* A prototyping encounter differs from the workings of a normal meeting, which might be scheduled with a known topic and a quantifiable agenda. You, on the other hand, don't know for certain what will happen. This difference is precisely your own goal of discovery. It is important to recognize this in order to authentically invite and engage an audience with your prototype experience.

Uncertainty while testing a prototype is something that you, as the curator of the experience, can anticipate—you can prepare to be surprised. Participants do not always have this benefit. This can create tension, reluctance, and even skepticism, expressed through common reactions:

> "You want me to do *what*?"

> "I don't understand how this works."

> "Is any of this helping you? Because I'm not really sure what we're doing."

Prototyping experiences benefit from two elements that Solomon calls "authentic entrance" and "authentic exit" framings. The entrance is an explicit benchmarking of what will happen, so that people can feel comfortable knowing what's next. The exit framing expands this intent through sharing how the participant's contribution specifically showed up or made a difference, as in, "Here's what we just did, and here are some things I learned and noticed." These basic mechanisms signal respect for someone who is contributing their time and attention to your experience and establish a participant as a teacher rather than a pawn in an experiment or a resource being mined. This is an entirely different proposition than the all-too-familiar (and rather disgusting) request to "pick someone's brain."

Ask the Right Questions

Here's how a prototype experience *is* like an interview. Having a plan or structure for asking questions will help focus your attention on a participant and away from yourself and your prototype. Just as a journalist does during an interview, prioritize your questions. Examine any assumptions you might have made in asking each question. If you're prototyping a new option for mobile banking, are you assuming that you'll be talking with people who have bank accounts? If you are prototyping a new voter registration process, are you assuming that someone is eligible to vote? Illuminating any assumptions ahead of time helps prioritize which questions to ask first.

Asking the right questions in context means getting beyond the binary options of yes and no. Even multiple-choice answers do very little to help you learn more about someone's perception beyond the boundaries of your question. Michael Barry, a designer and user-research expert, models research-based questions and conversations on the arc of a storyline. This is a helpful structure for formulating questions that develop a connection with a person, introduce an experience, and allow space to reflect on what it all means. By inviting people to participate while responding to questions and offering suggestions, you reinforce cooperative design (codesigning) as part of your prototyping process—working with participants as contributors rather than bystanders.

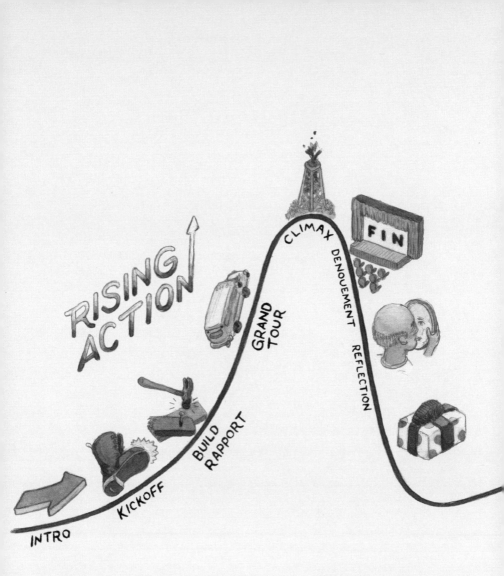

With your prototype, you have created a moment—an activity! Use that opportunity to ask people what they think and feel in response. Avoid using yes-or-no options, and consider a fundamental approach of asking open-ended questions, focusing on how and why as ways to get started.

How do you feel about this?

Is there something you would think about changing?

Can you tell me about the last time you experienced something like this?

Each of these is substantially different from:

Do you like this?

Would you buy this?

Is this easy or difficult?

It may seem simplistic to remind yourself to ask good questions as you seek feedback, but you may find yourself distracted by the fact that the conversation revolves around something that *you* made. Even professional designers become defensive when sharing their work for scrutiny. The best questions are valuable only if you are able to actually listen to people and understand their reactions. That really does take practice.

Focus on Feedback

For a comedian, feedback comes from laughter *and* silence. Both are clear cues about what works and what doesn't. The comedian can react in real time, but once the mic is off and the stand-up steps off stage, the show is over.

Anthropologist Margaret Mead described a different sort of feedback challenge for researchers doing work in the field:

> *Unlike the psychotherapist, who can restrict his total insights to the consulting room and turn them off altogether when dealing with members of his family and colleagues, such an anthropologist has to learn to be a whole person all of the time, twenty-four hours a day in the field and out of the field.*

This is closer to the reality of someone sharing prototypes for feedback. You are always "on." At times it may not be clear if the responses you are getting are good or bad, as would be obvious with laughter or silence. You will find fewer distinctions as answers become conversations instead of single words or statements. The most helpful information may come from indirect comments and observations that are not directly tied to your questions. This kind of feedback can come without warning, depending on the direction your prototype takes in real time, regardless of whether you're ready to respond.

Unlike a performer or someone offering analysis, you are uniquely a learner when sharing your work. This requires an approach closer to that of an observer who never knows what to expect but is prepared for it at any time. Tune your senses accordingly.

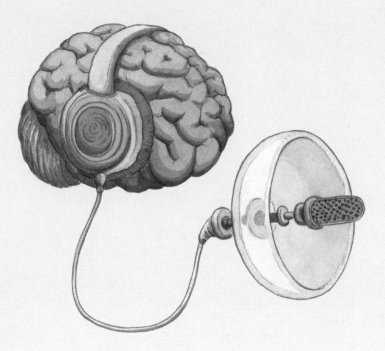

Observe Everything

Somebody beautiful walks into a bar or coffee shop or something, I don't look at the beautiful person. I look at the people looking at the beauty. That's where the fun is. That's where you see stuff you don't ordinarily see, which is someone dropping their mask.

—Leo Kottke, musician and observationalist

As you activate an experience, give yourself permission to perceive and learn without having to instantly draw conclusions from the unique circumstances that unfold. Make connections in the moment instead and quiet the conclusion. While watching a butterfly you can notice all the fluttery details—the unexpected hinging up and down, and the back-and-forth motions—and not feel responsible for understanding the physics of that delicate flight. For everything that you notice, you are not on the hook to understand its meaning in the moment. This is a practice in allowing connections to surface while separating curiosity from conclusion.

It helps to have a few guidelines in mind prior to engaging with people during prototyping so you don't get derailed by details in the moment. This includes establishing the protocols and procedures you hope to follow, such as letting your audience know that you would like to capture

notes, and adhering to the practice that audio and visual documentation, including photography (even quick shots and selfies!), can happen only with permission in response to a direct request. Ask people first, always.

There are many frameworks to help you categorize what you observe. When you are in the field and your prototype is in motion, consider these categories for your observations:

Patterns. What, if any, patterns or themes do you notice in how people are reacting and interacting? This includes people asking the same first question or having similar stumbling blocks on a feature or detail.

Senses. What are you noticing about how people are engaging? What do your senses communicate to you based on their response? Do you hear laughter? Is there something interesting about how people are touching or holding a device?

Analogies. Do you notice people identifying similar or dissimilar examples or experiences? Does someone say, "Hey, this is just like . . . but that is different because . . . "? Likewise, do *you* notice any new layers of information? What does this remind you of?

The Executive Education team at the Stanford d.school encourages the following categories to capture and sort observations:

Tensions. Tensions show up as conflicts or uneasiness in various categories. Is someone visibly reluctant to touch something? Are there issues—fit, finish, financial—that make a prototype or context somehow uncomfortable?

Contradictions. Contradictions often show up as differences between what people say and what they actually do. One benefit of a prototype experience is that you might have the opportunity to observe both—a "say" moment and a "do" moment—and follow up for further understanding.

Surprises. A surprise is a surprise. Make a note when you notice one. The real benefit here comes when you pay attention to instances that surprise you and surprise your prototyping audience. A great follow-up is "Hey, I was surprised when you did that. Can you tell me more about why you did that?"

Being an observer does not mean you must (or should) be a collector of secrets. From the simplest prototyping experience, you'll likely fill the preceding categories, or any that you choose to use, with observations, insights, and new questions. Share these observations and connections with the source! This means inviting the people you learned *from* into the position of people you learn *with,* as collaborators. Leadership consultants Jack Zenger and Joseph Folkman share a marker of good listening as *cooperative conversation*—the freedom people feel during a conversation to exchange information and observations as a way of reinforcing and helping each other. Sharing your observations for further understanding serves to affirm that you *are* hearing what another person is saying and that you are offering a response for their valued input.

Finally, don't forget to observe your own reactions. You can also consider yourself to be a valid audience. How do *you* react to an experience? Your behaviors and patterns during a prototype experience are important, too. Whether your work is self-focused or in service of others, a prototype is doing its job only when you are paying attention.

Time Your Work Wisely

"How long does it take to prototype something?" Students ask this question when figuring out how long it will take to complete an assignment, masking their more direct ask: *How much work is this going to take?* A different way to approach your work is considering how long it takes to answer a question. Organizational designers David Bland and Alex Osterwalder define prototype timing by asking "How much time do you have before you need to make a decision on what comes next?" This is a reminder to account for external forces that may drive your decisions.

Designing your timing is part of the politics of duration. Prototypes foreshadow change even though they may not represent a final situation—the change itself. That fact combines any preconceptions people have about change with the actual work you are trying to do. How long a prototype lasts will shape how people react to it: *permanent* can feel scary, while *temporary* feels tame. Matching the duration to intent is critical. Are you prototyping to understand a big and unexplored context, or are you prototyping to decide on a very specific feature? *Try eating as a vegetarian for a day, a week, a year.* Each of those time constraints serves the prototype objective of learning about a new behavior, but each one asks something different from the people participating in the prototype—yourself and others. Whether you intend it or not, your timing communicates a message.

Duration of a prototype experience can be timed by context instead of by clock. *Try eating as a vegetarian on your next vacation. Try eating as a vegetarian during an airport layover.* These are different ways to set constraints with a similar objective. The opportunity to learn *is* in real time, but there is unique value that comes from benchmark moments. While there is no definitive formula for this, you can do good work by starting with short durations to help reach the most minimal milestone before moving on to the next step or by pivoting with your objective based on what you learned in the meantime.

Mike Lydon and Anthony Garcia are urbanists and authors who prototype new ways of living in cities by rethinking public spaces, streets, utilities, and neighborhoods. These potentially massive changes start with scaled prototypes that use strategic timing. Lydon and Garcia created a technique called "48 × 48 × 48" to define a project testing cycle. The prototype starts with a very short duration (48 hours), followed by a longer next step (48 weeks), and then by a longer cycle (48 months). Each of these intervals is actually quick in the context of urban planning! They point out that the intervals are arbitrary, but the scale and staging of duration is deliberate. The intervals allow for phases of observation, reflection, and feedback, while also creating moments to pivot between intervals. Borrowing this concept of a (short) x (long) x (longer) experience and adding defined feedback and reflection points is a good way to approach timing a prototype.

Overshoot for Quality

"Quantity over quality, with caveats" is a solid ethos for prototyping success. A pine tree produces a billion pollen grains annually in an effort to reproduce even just one evergreen. (Any arborists care to fact check?) Overstated, yes, but over-pollination is a precedent. Great for trees! Lousy for people who sneeze. This is a lesson on quantity versus quality: in the context of prototyping, overshooting on quantity of prototype experiences can reduce the need for, and your reliance on, getting one "just right." At the same time, quantity without consideration of impact raises bigger questions about the quality of the investigator—you. *Achoo!*

Considering that caveat, mindfully working with multiple prototypes is a highly effective way to learn. Using different prototypes that all ask a similar question is one way to understand how people are reacting to the core question. It's a method for trying lots of different variations to see if a consistent trend or theme emerges even though the kinds of prototypes may vary.

In describing his trajectory of becoming a designer, Jason Mayden, former Air Jordan shoe designer at Nike, reacted to Michael Jordan's practice regimen: "As an athlete, he shoots a thousand free throws to practice. I'm going to do a thousand sketches as a designer." It's an easy takeaway that Mayden uses quantity of concepts as an intentional tool; he's hyper aware and deliberate about how it helps his practice.

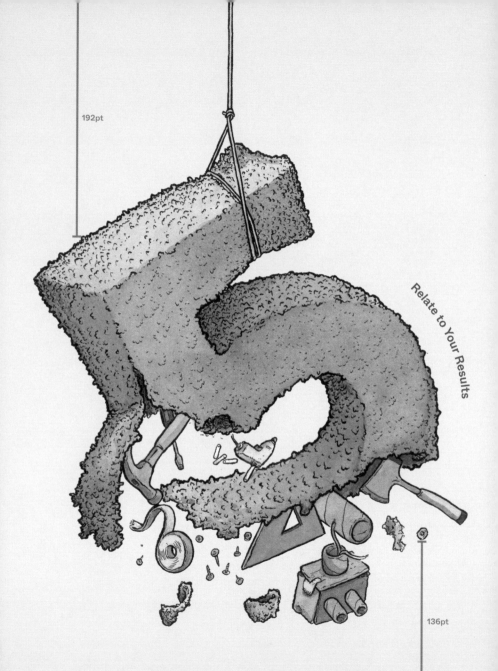

192pt

Relate to Your Results

136pt

C:7 M:7 Y:11 K:0

What Should I Make of This?

Sanchez Semibold 60pt

Prototyping is like a piñata: it becomes a success only after it has burst, creating the experience—and a sweet mess! The outcomes of prototyping can be cluttered and confusing, requiring some sense-making skills to help tell yourself and others what it all means. This is the deceptive aspect of making prototypes: it is about much more than the making. Creating prototype experiences requires you to relate to your results and reflect on your role. Only then can you determine whether—and if so, how, when, and why—you will take the next step with the learnings you've discovered.

Sanchez Semibold 9pt

C:100 M:40 Y:0 K:20

Explore the Outcomes

Anthropologist Laura Nader considers a conundrum faced by everyone about to embark on fieldwork: *Should I bring a problem with me or should I seek to find a focus?* Nader puts the prototyper on the spot, just as Bill Moggridge did with his distinction between designing something new or designing a new version of something. Do you consider your work a problem to be fixed? Do you understand your context well enough to see it as a problem or an opportunity? Your work began by asking yourself: *What do I think I'm doing?* That's a self-focused and necessary question to drive your engagement. With the results of an experience, you have a remarkable opportunity and maybe an obligation to continue that act of questioning: *Why should I continue doing this? What are the implications of carrying on this way? Who will feel the impact and what role did they have in shaping their own participation?* The results of the work you set into motion—your prototype experience—demand broader consideration: *How does this experience impact the world around me?*

The results of your work can fall into two categories: output and outcomes. These might seem interchangeable, but their differences are important. A basic way to differentiate output and outcome is to look at output as objective data, facts, and quantifiable information, whereas outcome consists of a qualified result with a subjective association, such as an emotional reaction, a hunch, or an unanticipated

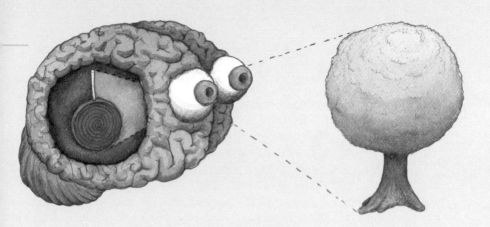

phenomenon. An output might be what someone *did* in response to a prototype, while an outcome might be how they *felt* about doing it and what they're *thinking* about now. For example, the output from an election might be the selection of a new official. An outcome of the same election might be renewed interest in campaign finance reform or changes in voter outreach strategies. Both are important categories for your findings because they have different implications for what you might choose to do next. The subsequent steps are determined by looking at results like this: I am *conscious* of this information/data/output, and I am *conscientious* about how my continued work with the outcomes may lead to unexpected situations.

Outcomes demand decisions. These can be active decisions or automatic choices—defaults. Based on what you learned, you might be excited to continue with your prototyping or change course. In short-term and self-impacting work this might be an easy or obvious choice to make. From a personal prototyping example of exploring new routes to work, you may have discovered that you enjoy the adventure of taking a new route every day, and going forward you'll choose adventure over efficiency for your commute. Cool! That's an easy outcome to put into action because it's personal—contained in your own sphere. As the outcomes from different and bigger prototypes grow more complex, you will face a choice about how to continue. Even though prototypes offer quick glimpses of new realities and new opportunities, it may take more time, effort, and commitment to understand the scale of what you've started to explore.

See(k) the Sneaky Realities of Scale

Scale relates to physical size and to the level of complexity in a prototyping experience. It's important to pay attention to intent and impact of scale early on because it is one of the most foreseeable traps for your resources. You may ask yourself *Did I go big enough with the experience? Not big enough? Did I miss something by not asking more people, making more prototypes, letting an experience last a little bit longer? Can I go bigger?* While big things sometimes require big prototypes, it's important to always aim your attention at behaviors of scale.

From a small prototype you might glimpse an opportunity to understand something at a larger scale. An example of exploring new options for bus stops might lead to learning about how public transit systems can better fit the lives of the people they serve. The magnitude shift from a basic bus stop can feel intimidating because it touches on abstract concepts and intervenes with the unknowns of big systems—people, infrastructure, economy, and all of the interwoven emotional threads. Complex concepts and systems can still be explored with prototypes. The approach is the same as with the small stuff, but with a greater awareness of how to stay on track. With a big prototype, each step will take more effort or require logistical details that can quickly derail you into focusing on a final

solution rather than keeping a question open. Bigger prototypes also require revisiting your connection to the work by asking yourself how you intend to approach the next steps and potential outcomes.

When Michael Tubbs was mayor of Stockton, California, he initiated the Stockton Economic Empowerment Demonstration (SEED). SEED is a city-scale prototype for exploring how a guaranteed income for Stockton citizens could demonstrate possibilities at a national scale. That is, Tubbs and his collaborators saw their roles as stewards of the local program to inform the question: What could this look like elsewhere? Even in its name, "Demonstration," it set an example for illuminating the protocols of prototyping at a large scale from the start.

The initial program details were distilled in the true spirit of a prototype: 125 residents each received $500 per month for eighteen months. The funds were distributed through debit cards and could be spent in any way the residents chose.

Stockton has a population of approximately 310,000, so while a group of 125 was a lot to manage, it still reflected a decision to keep the effort as low-resolution as possible. (This sample size compared to total population represents the same ratio as Stockton's population compared to the United States' total population.) The constraints—a limited number of people, limited duration, and parameters for payment amount, frequency, and format—helped to keep the prototype focused on the fundamental function.

The simplicity of these details doesn't distract from the fact that this is a *controversial* topic! Governance, governments, fears, hopes, and values are all embroiled in the context of the unknown: what would happen if such a system existed? This is a small-scale prototype to inform large-scale questions and concerns. Tubbs and his team identified several questions as objectives for informing the work. Among them:

How does this change a local economy?

How does this change the mindset of people receiving a guaranteed income?

How does this correlate to employment or unemployment?

How does the money get spent?

These are the kinds of questions that can stall in hypothetical projection at a local and national level. A muster that avoids the filibuster, the prototype informs these questions by mitigating fear of the unknown with actual answers to "what if" scenarios.

The SEED work took money. It took extensive community organizing. It required coordinating with more than a hundred participants and keeping that up for many months. These are details that require a lot of work. At first glance this may seem like going too high-res for the purpose of a prototype—investing too much time and energy into a concept, such that it will be hard to separate the emotional and financial investment from the potential outcomes. In the context of scale, however, these big details are actually very small steps compared to the concept being explored—universal income for more than three hundred million people. That is a really big idea with innumerable details to make it happen. The sneaky reality of scale is that big concepts still benefit from small prototypes, and small things can still require a lot of work. The concepts of (1) keeping resolution as low as possible and (2) using only the materials necessary to answer an early question both help people begin and manage big prototypes.

While it may feel intimidating to initiate a big prototype, the process is really an expanded implementation of familiar concepts. To envision a path toward and through a prototype, take inventory of what you already know how to do.

You already know to focus on critical objectives.

You know to prioritize early questions from later details.

You know to identify with an audience to ensure that your early work is going to be informative and collaborative.

This interim inventory can be both a reminder and an inspiration to approach the unknowns at any scale with focus instead of anxiety.

Mind the MacGuffin

"The MacGuffin" is an artifact from the film industry: it's an object or goal in a story with the sole purpose to set up the unfolding of the larger plot. Often the MacGuffin fades from further mention, disappearing in the context of a more important storyline. Was *Indiana Jones and the Last Crusade* really about finding the Holy Grail, or was that just a device to illuminate the relationship between Indy and his dad? Whether by intention or by accident, prototypes can act like a MacGuffin, sometimes drawing too much attention and other times successfully exposing outcomes. The MacGuffin conundrum is a reminder to pay attention as you prototype. Based on listening, learning, capturing, and perhaps pivoting a prototype in midstream, did you answer the question that started your quest or did you discover you were actually trying to learn something else along the way?

We can look to an example from the bike-share phenomenon of the 2010s to see how the meaning of a prototype can be tough to track as an experience unfolds. Citi Bike is a bike-sharing program started in New York City in 2011. It's a public-private venture with a corporate sponsor (Citibank) and a public sponsor (the City of New York). The program offers robust, rentable bikes at streetside stations around the city. The system is now a well-established operation, including the look and feel of the bikes, their locations within the city, and the mobile payment infrastructure.

An iteration of the bike service in New York expanded to San Francisco. The Ford GoBike program appeared identical in function, other than the new corporate and public sponsors—Ford Motor Company and the City of San Francisco, respectively. At the time, Ford had begun some internal experiments in civic spaces. These prototypes involved investing in rideshare and "public transportation" services in cities where car ownership was declining. The objective for these investigations shifted focus from selling cars to understanding more about the ways people move around in modern cities, with a hoped-for outcome of identifying opportunities beyond the company's current identity and product offerings. In San Francisco, Ford GoBike was one of those prototypes.

During the initial installation of services, stations seemed to pop up overnight, replacing street parking spaces, with some stations located far apart and others close together. Poor communication between the sponsors and the public about deciding where to locate stations and providing basic information about how to use the services led to growing distrust of the program. Public protest of the program management increased, with vandalism anticipated at each new installation. Bikes ended up stashed in alleys and tossed into local lakes. Morning commuters arrived at stations to find an entire fleet with flat tires—all slashed.

The combination of erratic installation and rampant vandalism forged a public sentiment that this system was not working as intended. Part of the problem appeared to come from contrast with precedents for success: this was a well-functioning product elsewhere, but why not in San Francisco? How were station locations picked? Why does the cycle station prioritize bikes over public parking? What does public space mean? Is this a for-profit enterprise being subsidized by the city? From a citizen's perspective it appeared that these questions had not been asked; as a result, the product became a misfit.

Here we find the MacGuffin. The function of the bike-sharing service shifted significance depending on who engaged it. For the corporate sponsor, the program was one of many prototypes used to understand a high-level objective. The plug-and-play precedent from a fully operational system in New York offered a quick way to get started. To the public sponsor, the program appeared to be a complete system, vetted by another municipality and ready for installation. To the public itself, the program felt less like a prototype to inform a future design and more like a forced-fit solution, implemented by the city with no attempts to understand this unique audience. As with these different entities, the perspectives from different people dictate whether work will feel like a success or a failure. This makes it especially difficult—and especially important—to decode how people who are impacted by your work consider its significance. A prototype that seems trivial to you may not be trivial at all to another audience that views the engagement with an entirely different meaning.

Prototype to Fail Well

When you make a thing, whatever that is, you become the designer. There it is: you are a prototype designer. Conflating prototypes and products is dangerous. They are not the same thing. With that approach, the first meal you cook could be your last! As a designer of prototypes, you can borrow a product design approach to guide your work: designing for failure. (Note that this is distinctly different from the nefarious practice of making home printers that break annually . . . to be replaced annually.)

Designing for failure is a practice of building failure into the useful function of a thing. Structural engineers specify building components to deform substantially before they collapse and ultimately fail. This depends on the building materials yielding before failure. That's not just casual talk. A concrete beam that supports a floor in a multi-story building—maybe you're on one right now?—is often designed to droop or sag as a way to signal that something is going wrong. As the materials yield, the beam communicates extrasensory information that people can see, feel, and hear, and it gives them time to react prior to catastrophe. That's a designed failure delivering an intentional outcome.

As the prototype designer that you are, consider this principle: prototype to fail well. (The concept of designing to fail feels too fatalistic for the otherwise optimistic practice of prototyping.) This principle borrows the convention of a product failing based on being either correct or incorrect. A prototype might appear to "fail" in the sense that if it was intended as a final product, it didn't correctly do its job. However, the value and ultimate success of failing with a prototype comes from transforming an early outcome into learning, which is not bound to that same spectrum of correct or incorrect or even the prototype itself. Fail well by making sense of early outcomes, asking *What did I learn and how did I learn it?* What you learned relates to the work you're doing—your questions, your objectives, and your discoveries. How you learned reflects your skills, intuition, and capacity for doing what you do. With every prototype you make, it's equally important to understand both what you learned and how you learned it. In that way, you can always find value from a "failed" prototype, unlike a failed product.

∘ ∘

Prototyping is a conduit for your curiosity. If you pay attention, it pays off with neat treats time after time: unforgettable lessons from totally forgettable forms. That's value created from ephemeral experiences, rather than from functional longevity or timeless beauty. Is this the ultimate unproduct? Maybe. With hope, *you* are the ultimate product of your prototyping practice: someone who asks questions with experiences and understands that answers are actually more questions in disguise.

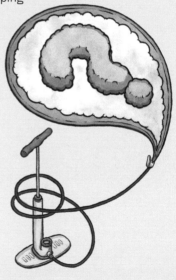

Acknowledgments

I share my gratitude for these people among so many:

Scott Doorley as The Finest. *Fin.*

The people who populate and perpetuate the d.school and make it unlike any other entity, anywhere.

Charlotte Burgess-Auburn, Bruce Boyd, and Kim Kendall-Humphreys, "The Wrecking Crew," whose contributions toward defining the d.school community cannot be overstated.

+

Jennifer Brown for her exquisite personal concern and her ability to anchor this work while seeing it into yet unscripted directions.

Scott Teplin for opening his art to this opportunity.

Kim Keller, Annie Marino, and everyone at Ten Speed Press for their dedicated work.

+

Intrepid students everywhere, including Stanford University, The University of Texas at Austin, Tokyo Institute of Technology, and Waseda University.

+

Sandra Olive Price Witthoft for tirelessly trying new things.

My family and friends for everything.

Contributors

I gratefully acknowledge the following for their contributions through personal communication, example, and inspiration:

Purin Phanichphant
Jon Freach
Verena Paepcke-Hjeltness
Erica Estrada-Liou
Matt Brezina
Natasha Blum
Blaine Merker
John Bela
Carissa Carter
Joe Romano
Emily Pilloton-Lam
Adam Royalty
David Janka
Michael Barry
Lisa Kay Solomon
Joe Mellin

Jesse Silver
David Goligorsky
Dan O'Sullivan
Louis Schump
Jason Chua
Deborah Carter
Victor Saad
Grace Stanat
Adam Selzer
Molly Wilson
Susie Wise
Kate Canales
Thomas Both
Sarah Stein-Greenberg
Bernie Roth
David Kelley

Photographs and images courtesy of:

Stanford d.school, page 47
San Francisco Museum of
    Modern Art, page 47
Money Mark, page 49
Michael Dunn/Lonesoulsurfer,
    page 49
Natalie Whearley, page 51
Scott Doorley, page 51
Carissa Carter, page 53
Creative Commons, pages
    53, 83

Joe Romano, page 55
Natasha Blum/The Emergency
    Design Collective, page 57
John Entwistle, pages 67–68
Adam Royalty, page 75
David Janka and
    CompactCath, pages 76–77
Blaine Merker and John Bela,
    page 81

All others by the author.

Sources

For references and further resources regarding materials, please visit: **dschool.stanford.edu/books/thisisaprototype**

Index

Published in the United States by Ten Speed Press, an imprint of
Random House, a division of Penguin Random House LLC, New York.
TenSpeed.com
RandomHouseBooks.com

Ten Speed Press and the Ten Speed Press colophon are registered trademarks
of Penguin Random House LLC.

Scissor illustration on cover © 4zevar - stock.adobe.com

Typefaces: Hope Meng's d.sign, Dinamo's Whyte, and LatinoType's Sanchez

Library of Congress Cataloging-in-Publication Data
Names: Witthoft, Scott, author.
Title: This is a prototype : the curious craft of building new ideas /
    Scott Witthoft ; illustrations by Scott Teplin.
Description: First edition. | California : Ten Speed Press, 2022. |
    Includes index.
Identifiers: LCCN 2021029925 (print) | LCCN 2021029926 (ebook) |
    ISBN 9781984858047 (trade paperback) | ISBN 9781984858054 (ebook)
Subjects: LCSH: Creative thinking. | Imagination.
Classification: LCC BF408 .W58 2022 (print) | LCC BF408 (ebook) |
    DDC 153.3/5—dc23
LC record available at https://lccn.loc.gov/2021029925
LC ebook record available at https://lccn.loc.gov/2021029926

Trade Paperback ISBN: 978-1-9848-5804-7
eBook ISBN: 978-1-9848-5805-4

Printed in China

Acquiring editor: Hannah Rahill | Editor: Kim Keller
Designer: Annie Marino | Art director: Emma Campion
Production designers: Mari Gill and Faith Hague
Production manager and prepress color: Jane Chinn
Copyeditor: Kristi Hein | Proofreader: Lisa Brousseau | Indexer: Ken DellaPenta
Publicist: David Hawk | Marketer: Windy Dorresteyn
d.school creative team: Scott Doorley, Charlotte Burgess-Auburn,
    and Jennifer Brown

10 9 8 7 6 5 4 3 2 1

First Edition